POISED FOR
SUCCESS

ALSO BY JACQUELINE WHITMORE

Business Class: Etiquette Essentials for Success at Work

POISED FOR SUCCESS

MASTERING THE FOUR QUALITIES
THAT DISTINGUISH OUTSTANDING
PROFESSIONALS

JACQUELINE WHITMORE

St. Martin's Press
New York

POISED FOR SUCCESS: MASTERING THE FOUR QUALITIES THAT DISTINGUISH OUT-
STANDING PROFESSIONALS. Copyright © 2011 by Jacqueline Whitmore. Fore-
word copyright © 2011 by Victoria Moran. All rights reserved. Printed in
the United States of America. For information address St. Martin's Press,
175 Fifth Avenue, New York, N.Y. 10010.

www.stmartins.com

Design by Elina D. Nudelman

Library of Congress Cataloging-in-Publication Data

Whitmore, Jacqueline.
  Poised for success : mastering the four qualities that distinguish
outstanding professionals / Jacqueline Whitmore.—1st ed.
     p. cm.
  ISBN 978-0-312-60032-7
  1. Business etiquette.   2. Professional employees—Conduct of life.
3. Success.   I. Title.
  HF5389.W485 2011
  650.1—dc23

                                     2011025862

First Edition: November 2011

10   9   8   7   6   5   4   3   2   1

This book is dedicated with love, light, and gratitude
to my husband and best friend,
Brian Gleason,
for loving me and all of my imperfections,

and to my precious canine companion and fur child,
Oliver,
for being the embodiment of love and loyalty,
and for patiently teaching me how to take breaks, play often,
and always live in the moment.

CONTENTS

PART THREE:

PROFESSIONALISM

PART FOUR:

PASSION

FOREWORD

I was introduced to Jacqueline Whitmore's work (and, ultimately, to Jacqueline Whitmore) through her first book, *Business Class*. I studied it so thoroughly that I had to buy a second copy to replace the one that had grown illegibly underlined and highlighted. I learned so much from *Business Class* that I wondered what a new book could add to the topic of etiquette and decorum for contemporary professionals. In *Poised for Success,* however, Whitmore goes from protocol to principle, from expected courtesy to the exceptional caring. This is the difference between the person who tries to beat down the door to success and the one for whom it opens easily as a matter of course.

This is etiquette for the twenty-first century, and it's far less about dusty rules than about developing genuine respect for oneself and others. *Poised for Success* comes at the perfect time. We're living in an era rife with upheavals at various points around the globe, and round-the-clock media chronicling each one of them. It can feel as if, other than sending a check to this charity and that fund and some relief effort or other, we're powerless to affect the state of our world. But that's not entirely true: we can treat those around us in ways that make them feel better about themselves, and start a ripple effect that can spread farther than we know.

In earlier decades, etiquette was the purview of the privileged and books on the subject made this clear. When I was eleven or twelve, I ordered an imposing tome on the topic from the Book-of-the-Month Club and was fascinated to discover that I was to greet the Queen of England in a far different way than I would a mere duchess or earl. The only problem was, we didn't get a lot of royalty in Kansas City, so that book read more like fiction or fantasy than as a guide for relating to the real human beings who populated my life. This is where *Poised for Success* shines.

Jacqueline Whitmore is a real human being, and she shares in this book her humble beginnings, the lessons she learned from her mother and from the variety of jobs that brought her, rung after rung, to the top-of-the-ladder post she holds today as founder and director of The Protocol School of Palm Beach and a foremost authority on business etiquette. She didn't get there by simply knowing which fork to use at a formal dinner, although she knows that, as well. Her secret, as I see it, is twofold: First, learn what's expected and do that, because the externals, the details, the little things, do matter. And second, be interested in the person you're with, whether face-to-face, on the phone, or via e-mail. This is equal-opportunity interest, whether you're in the company of your boss, a glittering celebrity, or an anonymous stranger doing a job you know wasn't the one he or she aspired to when asked as a child, "What do you want to be when you grow up?"

There's no shortage of instruction out there on what it takes to succeed, but Jacqueline's approach is one that works without asking us to win through intimidation or practice some mental wizardry that promises to render us rich, famous, and powerful. Instead, she provides practical tools we can use today to place a higher value on ourselves, our gifts, and the people around us. She shows us how to leverage our knowledge, skills, and uniqueness to provide our company, our customer, or the world at large with something too beneficial to pass up.

So, enjoy yourself. You're about to read a delightful and helpful book with suggestions you'll start putting into practice before you're halfway through. Expect as a result to like yourself a little more, get along better with everybody (even the difficult people), and realize before too long that you've developed instincts about what is indeed "the next right action," when to speak up, when to press "send," and when to wait, poised, for success.

—VICTORIA MORAN, author of *Creating a Charmed Life*

INTRODUCTION

LUCK IS WHAT HAPPENS WHEN PREPARATION MEETS OPPORTUNITY.

— SENECA, ROMAN PHILOSOPHER

How does one compete in today's competitive job market when there are so many bright, capable people out there? The hard truth is that the ones who get ahead are often those who are able to muster enough courage to take risks and connect from the heart.

Between your desire to succeed, your ability to recognize opportunity, and your willingness to take action (especially if it holds some risk), you have the potential to alter the course of your career. That's how success happens. There often isn't a straight line between where you are now and where you want to be; the road may be winding, rocky, or rough, but it's there. The pathway is called *ambition* and it leads to success.

Success doesn't happen by accident. It happens by design. Successful people aren't smarter than everyone else. They just practice more than their peers. Hall of Fame basketball player Ed Macauley once said, "When you are not practicing, remember, someone somewhere is practicing, and when you meet him he will win." Successful people are willing to take advantage of opportunities that come their way and they keep on moving toward what they want, sometimes in big strides but mostly in small steps that ultimately make a difference. To become better at anything, whether it's sports, music, or building better business relationships, you must practice often. Whether you're working toward a career goal or the dream of one day owning your own business, this book can help you move closer to your vision by showing you how to connect with others who can help you get there, but you have to practice.

When I wrote my first book, *Business Class: Etiquette Essentials for Success at Work*, I included stories and examples of why "soft" skills (communication, diplomacy, and good manners), once considered the "soft" stuff, are now the hard stuff. The book was a huge success; however, there's more to being your best self than knowing how to properly shake hands or wield a knife and fork. That's why I decided to write this book.

Poised for Success is less about etiquette and protocol and more about how to build longer-lasting, more meaningful relationships and how to put others first in your life. By learning how to cultivate four personal qualities—***presence, polish, professionalism,*** and ***passion***—you can propel yourself toward success, however you may define it. Success is as much the journey as it is the destination. The purpose of this book is to make that journey, *your* journey, a mindful and meaningful process.

Reading this book is an investment in yourself; it will help you do all you can to prepare yourself for the moments when opportunity knocks on your door. By putting these four uncommon qualities into common practice you'll open yourself up to circumstances you might otherwise have missed or simply passed by. You'll be in a position where you can enhance your relationships, expand your horizons, and move forward to the next level of your career with confidence. You'll be poised for success!

PART ONE

PRESENCE

CHAPTER I

Poise Is Presence Personified

**GIVE THE WORLD THE BEST YOU HAVE, AND
THE BEST WILL COME BACK TO YOU.**
— ELLA WHEELER WILCOX, AUTHOR AND POET

Whenever you have an unusual job, particularly if you're a circus clown, crematory operator, snake charmer, or etiquette expert, people make assumptions about your personality and background. In my case, I *am* an etiquette expert, and many people I meet today assume that I grew up enjoying a privileged lifestyle. But nothing could be further from the truth.

I was born the fourth of five children in the small town of Haines City, located in Central Florida. My mom, Elsie, left my abusive, alcoholic father (her third husband) when I was just five years old. Unable to support all of us on her own, Mom had to make the heartbreaking choice of sending my three older siblings to live with their father. My mother, my younger brother, and I moved in with my Granny Johnson until Mom could afford a down payment on a government-subsidized house she found in a quaint middle-class neighborhood.

Growing up, I didn't attend fancy tea parties, cotillions, or private schools. Life was more than modest; my clothes came from discount stores or I dressed in my cousin's hand-me-downs. The special activities many of my friends enjoyed, including dance classes, piano lessons, and summer vacations, were simply out of the question. I was raised Southern Baptist and spent most of my childhood in church, where I learned to sing and play handbells.

Because my dad was a World War II disabled veteran, I was fortunate to attend college thanks to the educational funding I received from the Veterans Benefits Administration. I majored in broadcasting at the University of Florida with the intent to become a TV reporter. But my career aspirations quickly fizzled when I took an internship with CNN in Washington, D.C. Unfortunately, I loathed every minute of it and realized that I wasn't cut out for the cutthroat radio and TV industry.

After graduation, I had no idea what I wanted to be when I grew up, so I explored a variety of unique and diverse occupations. I was a sales associate for ladies' clothes at an upscale department store, a singer, dancer, and actor at SeaWorld of Florida, an administrative assistant and special events coordinator at the Walt Disney World Dolphin Resort, and a flight attendant with Northwest Airlines.

I found happiness in every job I had and I never imagined that life could get even better... until I landed my dream job in 1993. That's when I had the good fortune to be hired as the assistant director of public relations for one of the most luxurious and exclusive hotels in the world—The Breakers in Palm Beach, Florida. Listed on the National Register of Historic Places, the hotel has played host to generations of the rich and famous. My job at the prestigious and palatial Breakers Hotel was a portal into a glamorous, glittery, and elegant world. It was also my finishing school. Who knew that one day this small-town girl would dine and dance at some of the most opulent charity galas in the world or rub elbows with people she read about in magazines and newspapers? As time went on, I eventually took part in The Breakers Annual Executive Etiquette Camp and then went on to take a more extensive business etiquette certification course in Washington, D.C. As a result, I was named the hotel's first protocol officer, which afforded me the opportunity to mix and mingle with some of the world's most interesting and influential people who came to Palm Beach.

What Presence Is and What It Is Not

The Merriam-Webster dictionary defines presence as "a noteworthy quality of poise and effectiveness." Poise is all about balance—the way you hold yourself and how you move through the world. It's about paying attention to the details of you, which means accepting, embracing, and taking full advantage of all you have to work with. It's your desire to improve, without the fear of embarrassment or intimidation.

The Palm Beach lifestyle could have easily intimidated me, but my sheer desire to be a part of this exciting world helped me quell any hesitation or discomfort I felt. I learned to cultivate my presence and adapt and assimilate into my surroundings just as a chameleon blends in with its environment. I loved working at The Breakers, but like all good things, my tenure there eventually came to an end.

My mother often said, "A person's life can change in an instant with just one phone call or trip to the mailbox," and she was correct. On a hot, sticky afternoon in August 1998, I unsuspectingly received a phone call that changed my life. My boss called me and in a curt voice he instructed me to report to his office immediately. When I hung up the phone, I broke out into a cold sweat—the kind you get right before someone tells you some really bad news. When I entered my boss's office, my heart sank when I saw the director of human resources sitting next to him. My suspicions were immediately confirmed—my job position was about to be eliminated.

I sat there, calm and composed, but on the inside I felt rage and disappointment. My husband and I had only been married two months; we had a mortgage, car payments, wedding bills, and other financial obligations. But rather than focus on the "failure" aspects of this experience, I decided to stay poised and face my adversity with grace. A month later, I decided to take the plunge and start my own business—The Protocol School of Palm Beach, a company that's still going strong today.

Whenever you can stay centered and embrace your own poise during tough times, you tap into your most precious inner resources—insight, strength, and depth of character. Presence has its own power source. When you're composed, sufficiently practiced, and self-assured, when you feel strong enough to move mental mountains, you are poised for success.

Most of the greatest achievers in the world, from entrepreneurs to athletes and artists, could not have achieved their levels of success without experiencing some adversity. For example, swimmer and Olympic gold medalist Michael Phelps has athletic poise and presence. During competitions, he has the ability to develop and maintain a particular state of physical and psychological readiness, both of which he can summon on demand.

Whether you're an athlete, astronaut, business owner, or employee, presence is a prerequisite to peak performance. Some people consider presence an innate gift or inborn talent, such as the ability to carry a tune or draw a picture, but anyone can cultivate this quality. It's simply the ability to develop an internal sense of serenity or centeredness, a state of mind that brings enormous peace and inner strength. It's the ability to put yourself in a state of mind where calmness and power intertwine (think extreme self-confidence), allowing you to stand out, perform at your peak, and outshine the competition!

Presence isn't something you put on in the morning and take off in the evening; it's a part of your essence. Once it's internalized, it emanates from within, replacing self-doubt and anxiety with self-empowerment. Others are drawn to you because you exude a "humble" self-confidence and optimism. It's evident that you have something special to offer. In this book I explain how to achieve that "special something."

Professionals who possess presence are confident without arrogance, composed without stiffness, and kind without pretension, to friends and strangers alike. They are able to express their graciousness with everyone they meet, from corporate leaders to custodians.

When you cultivate your own presence you draw admiration from others. Not only will people want to develop friendships with you; they also will want to socialize with you, do business with you, and, in some instances, maybe even date and marry you. (Don't laugh . . . it happened to me.)

CHAPTER 2

Package Yourself for Success

WHEN YOUR IMAGE IMPROVES, YOUR PERFORMANCE IMPROVES.

— ZIG ZIGLAR, BESTSELLING AUTHOR AND MOTIVATIONAL SPEAKER

In life, just as in school, we are graded by others. But instead of test scores, we are "graded" on our appearance. The good news about this covert social classroom is that every time you dress well you earn extra credit. Why? Because the way we dress and the way we carry ourselves can communicate to others that we are competent, knowledgeable, elegant, gracious, or powerful, or possess any other quality we choose to convey. It helps to consciously consider the kind of image or ability you wish to present to a particular "audience" because this is something you have control over. And who doesn't love to be in control?

In less than thirty seconds, we form opinions about others based solely on visual cues. This is such a common practice we're often not aware of the reactions or judgments we make based on someone's appearance and bearing. If you have any doubts about this, the next time you're seated in an airplane observe other passengers as they board. You'll realize that you're assessing each individual and maybe even deciding whom you'd like (or not like) to take the seat beside you.

Think back on previous flights and recall the people you've avoided talking to as well as those with whom you've initiated conversations during flights. Most likely there have been times when you were disappointed or even a bit disgusted at the bedraggled or unbecoming person who sidled in next to you. Some travelers instinctively place a handbag, book, or briefcase on the next seat in an effort to send a silent "Do not sit here" message.

Like it or not, human beings tend to be somewhat superficial at times and tend to favor good-looking, well-turned-out people. From job candidates to those we date or choose as life partners, looks are a compelling factor in our selection. Even in the animal kingdom, females are more sexually attracted to males with the strongest, most beautiful, exaggerated features.

Of course, it would be ideal if we were all judged for our intelligence and experience rather than our style and looks, but research indicates otherwise. Before we ever open our mouths to speak, people have already formed an opinion about our educational level, personality, career level, personal competence, and more. According to Dr. Mona Phillips, a sociology professor at Spelman College in Atlanta, studies continue to verify that attractive or good-looking people have distinct advantages over plain or homely individuals. Citing research (pioneered by K. Dion, E. Berscheid, and G. Walster) on the "halo effect," Dr. Phillips explains that many interviewers assume that if a candidate is physically attractive, then he or she must possess other good qualities, too. Phillips describes the halo effect as "a clustering of assumed positive attributes based on one's appearance."

Dr. Alvin F. Poussaint, a renowned psychiatry professor

and faculty dean for student affairs at Harvard Medical School, believes that people generally like to be around attractive people because of their physical appeal. In the article "Do Attractive People Get Better Treatment than Others," published by *Jet* (September 3, 2001), Dr. Poussaint explains that even small children differentiate between playmates who are attractive and those who are unattractive (and while some of this may stem from fairy tales, let's remember that even babies are exposed to TV and commercial images that drive the message home). "People tend to think that those with attractive looks are more trustworthy or honest than people who are unattractive," suggests Dr. Poussaint.

On the other hand, he also admits that being too good-looking doesn't always work in one's favor, suggesting that extremely attractive people can stir up jealousies in others who then may reject them. At work, a woman who is drop-dead gorgeous may sometimes be perceived as less intelligent than her average-looking counterparts. She may have difficulty being taken seriously, especially by men, and end up being a source of resentment or envy by other women.

Yet, with few exceptions, the attractiveness factor persists. Dr. Frederick Work, Jr., a plastic and reconstructive surgeon from Atlanta, Georgia, posits that attractive people receive special treatment and there are more opportunities available to them. He points out that because our society regards attractiveness so highly, it's almost a given that more and more people will opt for cosmetic surgical procedures. But before you break out your credit card and start looking for a qualified plastic surgeon, it's important to know that regardless of what nature did or didn't give you, it's possible to enhance your appearance without having a nip or tuck or spending a fortune.

THE TOP FOUR EXCUSES FOR NOT LOOKING YOUR BEST

We all have our reasons for not stepping up to the plate and investing in ourselves from time to time. Here are some of the more common excuses for not looking our best:

1. **"I'm too busy."** In today's world of multitasking and multiple family demands, "appearance" often takes a backseat to necessities such as commuting, working, and caring for children and/or aging parents. Tight budgets can make dental visits, clothing purchases, hair maintenance, cosmetics, or self-care products low priorities in the face of house and utility payments or other financial obligations. You may often wake up tired and uninspired, but you don't have to flaunt it. You only have one body, and you want it to last as long as possible. You only have one life, and you want to be the best "you" you can possibly be. We all know that when we look good we feel better about ourselves and others treat us better. This may sound like a stretch, but holding to high standards of appearance every day is an investment in being happier, healthier, and more successful in our work. Living in a visually oriented society such as ours places physical presentation on a par with our work presentations, and in this competitive marketplace no one can afford to send an inconsistent message. Looking your best isn't about vanity; it's about self-investment.

2. **"I'm a casual type."** The definition of "casual" has reached an all-time low in our society. I'll admit that from time to time I, too, will throw on the first thing that's within grabbing distance and, since I work at home, I often live in faded yoga pants, flip-flops, and T-shirts, the ultimate in casual. I usually reserve makeup

and a hairstyle for when I meet with a client or have a speaking engagement. Just so you know, when I go out into the business world I strive to look my best; as I work in the etiquette business, people expect me to look and act a certain way, and I do my best to live up to their expectations, as well as my own.

Regardless of what type of business you're in, your overall appearance speaks volumes about you. Granted, there may be jobs where looking disheveled or poorly groomed is acceptable, but they are few and far between, if, indeed, they exist at all.

3. **"I can't afford to be fashionable."** Keeping up with fashion can be costly, but you can always be stylish, even on a budget. True style comes from within; it's an extension of your personality. You want a wardrobe comprised of items that fit, flatter, and add a dash of flair. Choose clothes that make sense for the life you lead, but keep an eye on your future career goals and dress accordingly. You don't need quantity, so invest in quality. Build your wardrobe around a core of timeless classic pieces rather than wasting money on tempting trendy items. From there you can systematically spruce up your wardrobe around central garments. I learned a long time ago that quality clothing lasts longer and can be amortized over the years to mere pennies per wearing. To stretch your wardrobe dollars, take advantage of the after-holiday sales; you might end up with two or three outfits for the price of one. If you find a designer whose styles work for you, over time you can craft personal touches to your appearance. With a little bit of money and creativity and a lot of consistency, you'll build a wardrobe that will make you proud.

4. **"I have no style."** If you've ever lamented about your seeming lack of style, relax. None of us is born with a "style" gene.

Don't get discouraged if you make some fashion mistakes along the way. We all do.

After graduating from college, I wanted to broaden my horizons, so I applied for a management trainee position with a major hotel chain in New York City. I was tired of Florida and wanted to spread my wings and experience life in the big city. I was thrilled when the human resources manager invited me to the Big Apple for an interview. I went to my closet and excitedly pulled out my one and only business outfit—my creamy tweed suit and seashell-pink polyester blouse. To complete my ensemble, I chose my sheer, cream-colored panty hose and matching pumps, accented with little bows (yes, *bows*). Proudly sporting my well-coordinated attire, I felt ready for anything.

When I landed at LaGuardia Airport, I gathered my bags and stepped outside to catch a cab. The minute I hit the sidewalk, my heart sank. There I stood, in my Florida pink flamingo ensemble, surrounded by hundreds of people dressed from head to toe in every imaginable variation of black. I gasped, realizing that I looked like I was dolled up for a tea party instead of a job interview. It was a crushing, unforgettable experience. In retrospect, I'm not the least bit surprised that I didn't get the job.

I blame my poor judgment on youthful naïveté but also on the fact that image seminars were rare in the eighties and so were fashion role models unless you watched popular TV shows like *Dynasty, Dallas,* and *Miami Vice,* all of which influenced how a lot of people dressed during that decade. I learned a memorable lesson about diligently doing research and dressing appropriately for the industry and its environment on that fateful day. Maybe my story will help you prevent a similar fashion disaster.

DRESS FOR YOUR INDUSTRY

The way you dress for work has probably been influenced—if not determined—by your industry. For example, if you work in a creative career such as graphic arts, entertainment, or the high-tech world, you can usually wear clothes that are on the casual, funky, or fashion-forward side. If you work in a more conservative industry such as banking, finance, insurance, accounting, law, health care, academia, politics, social work, counseling, or civil service, you're better off wearing conservative clothing that doesn't scream, "Look at me!" In other words, pay attention to the people around you (especially those one or two levels above your position) and choose outfits that enhance your appearance with a purpose. Even if you have little or no face-to-face contact with clients or customers, it makes good business sense to respect your internal customers (and, most important, yourself) by dressing in ways that hint of being competent and caring about your job.

DRESS FOR YOUR CLIENT'S COMFORT ZONE, NOT YOUR OWN

When you are choosing clothing, your first criterion should be comfort, but here's an aspect you may not have considered: the comfort factor is actually for others instead of yourself. Whether your aim is landing a job or promotion, a contract, or a new professional ally, make it a priority to help the other person feel comfortable with you. This is another way of saying *dress for the occasion*. For example, if you work in a creative career, but most of your clients are attorneys, they will feel more at ease if you're similarly dressed. Save the casual slacks, wild tie, or strappy shoes for an evening on the town with your friends.

Before any job interview or meeting with an important client, research a company's image, office environment, and internal values so you can avoid anything similar to my New York fashion fiasco. Dorothy Waldt, a partner in the retail practice with CTParners, a global retained executive search firm, headquarted in New York City, recalls a candidate who was sent to interview with a retailer that had a very casual fashion ethos. Unfortunately, the job seeker dressed up. "The clothes that he was wearing were so polar opposite of what the company did that they thought he just didn't get them at all," says Waldt. Based solely on his attire, they never even bothered to interview him. "He sat in a holding room for seven hours and then flew home." A little research might have helped him land the job. The rule of thumb is to always dress for the occasion and the client's emotional comfort.

OCCASIONALLY WEED OUT YOUR WARDROBE

Still wearing that treasured, tattered Grateful Dead concert T-shirt from decades ago? As painful as it might be, now is the time to retire it; give it a new life as a rag for washing your car or cleaning mirrors. I'm not saying you need to get rid of all your old clothes, just the ones that make you look like you're suspended in a time warp. Keep whatever works: tops that look good and fit well, your solid-color or simple-print cashmere sweaters, and classic trousers, suits, and any items you regularly wear.

Here's a wardrobe rule to live by: If you haven't worn it in over a year, dump it or donate it. If you're holding on to a piece of clothing that no longer fits, get rid of it. Maybe you'll lose those extra pounds; maybe you won't. But by then, it will probably be too old to look good, too out of style, or too ill fitting, so say goodbye to it. In short, keep your wardrobe current and in good shape (just like you).

THERE'S PUTTING ON CLOTHES AND THERE'S GETTING DRESSED

Dressing is an art that provides you with an opportunity to creatively express yourself each and every day. It's your personalized method of nonverbally presenting yourself to the world.

If you want to be thought of as "well dressed" by those around you, here are three guidelines: make classic wardrobe choices, create a consistent personal style, and opt for an appearance that appropriately matches the occasion, from office attire to after-hour business events.

I'd like to add that it helps to dress well when you travel, because you never know whom you might meet in an airport or on a plane. And to make special occasions more special, I encourage you to take it up a notch or two for a ballet, opera, or Broadway show and other social occasions that once called for getting dressed up.

INVEST IN A FEW INVESTMENT PIECES

No matter how your wardrobe evolves, expands, or retracts, I encourage both men and women to purchase a few basic investment pieces. If you get spooked by sticker shock when you consider such an undertaking, remember that classic, high-quality clothing lasts a long time and never goes out of style.

Use the "cost-per-wearing" amortizing method to calculate the true long-term cost of any wardrobe item. Divide the number of times you plan to wear the item by the initial cost and you will get the cost per wearing.

For example, let's say you spend $1,000 for a classic overcoat. It will cost you approximately $11.11 per wearing to wear that coat for 90 days. It will cost you approximately $2.22 if you wear it for 450 days. As you can see, the price will be an even bigger bargain if you wear it for many, many years.

Seek Out a Personal Shopper

For some of us, the very thought of clothes shopping (especially for those long-lasting classic, quality items) can be almost as daunting as enduring a root canal. What are your options if you don't like to (or haven't the time) to shop? The answer is outsourcing. Many stores now employ personal shoppers who can make your consumer life much easier and more enjoyable. This person will meet with you to assess your body type and will discuss your style preferences, financial parameters, and other considerations. Once your personal shopper knows your profile, he or she will make suggestions and help you find just the right garments to fit your personal taste or occasion, all within your schedule and budget. This person will shop for you and then present the items for your review in a private fitting room at the store. If the store is truly upscale, the personal shopper will present his or her choices while you sip sparkling water from a crystal glass or drink freshly brewed coffee from a china cup.

The best part: this service is free and there is no minimum purchase required. The personal shopper is paid by the department store and is there to help make your shopping experience easier and more pleasurable. The option of working with a personal shopper is an especially good fit for a shopaholic who has too little time and too little restraint or a shopping-phobic person who has too little patience and imagination to select the right items.

If you haven't yet had the pleasure of working with a personal shopper, I recommend it, if for nothing else, just for the experience. You may also want to invest in a certified image consultant. This person is trained to help you look your best, from head to toe. To find an image consultant in your area, contact the Association of Image Consultants International (www.aici.org). Imagine the convenience of having someone else share the responsibility of helping you perfectly package yourself, professionally or personally; it's all yours for the asking.

CHAPTER 3

The Well-Dressed Man

CLOTHES MAKE THE MAN. NAKED PEOPLE HAVE LITTLE
OR NO INFLUENCE ON SOCIETY.

— MARK TWAIN, AUTHOR AND HUMORIST

Fred Astaire, the iconic dancer, singer, and actor, was not exactly what you might consider strikingly handsome. He was short, slightly built, and if dressed in the casual clothes of today he might not have stood out in a crowd. A few critics might even have thought he was downright goofy-looking, but astute women such as Audrey Hepburn had a different opinion. When the famous actress was asked if she considered Astaire "good-looking," Hepburn replied, "I think so, because charm is the best-looking thing in the world, isn't it?"

Fred Astaire's ordinary looks were greatly enhanced by his wardrobe; he definitely personified the phrase "clothes make the man." What he wore onstage and in front of a camera became part of his image arsenal; he always looked dapper and distinguished. Astaire's sense of style came from his fearlessness to try new things such as his classic gambit of substituting a brightly patterned tie for a belt. When he wasn't sporting his

trademark top hat and tails on stage and screen, Astaire pre-
ferred to wear softer, casual clothing. (Think roomy trousers and
sweaters in lightweight fabrics that hung so effortlessly.) In Fred
Astaire's world, wearing unstructured, generously cut clothing
never meant sacrificing a sense of refinement.

Style is something you develop from within. When you look
at the way Astaire dressed, the best thing about him was that he
never made it look self-conscious. You have to practice to make it
look unpracticed, so to speak.

Even today, there are several important lessons we can learn
from Fred Astaire, and they can be applied to any man's lifestyle.
If you want to use what I call the Astaire Influence, everything
you wear must appear casual and effortless. For example, if you
wear a suit every day, go for the kind of fit and fabric that makes
you look and feel almost as comfortable as if you were wearing
golf slacks or even jeans and a T-shirt. Despite his tailored dance
suits with slim, high armholes, Astaire could practically do cart-
wheels even in white-tie attire.

If you are the relaxed type, you can follow Astaire's lead by
making sure that you always look polished. This is where correct
fit (even your T-shirts) is critical so your clothes will hang properly on your body whether you're moving or standing still. Like
Fred Astaire, be willing to take some risks so you can develop
your own style.

Astaire was ahead of his time, and he embraced pattern and
color in everything he wore, from plaid sports jackets to bright
blue socks. Sometimes, Astaire topped off his ensembles with a
boutonniere in his lapel or a silk pocket square while wearing
suede shoes. He had a way of adding a sense of flair to his personal style, and you can, too.

Astaire's philosophy still rings true even today: you don't have to be a slave to fashion. In fact, being too fashion forward can be a distraction in more conservative business settings. Instead, find out what looks good on you, and if your clothing is well cut and well made, no one will ever accuse you of being out of style.

Dressing well rests on two pillars: color and proportion. Once you learn which colors enhance your complexion and why specific proportions flatter your physique, you are halfway home. If what you wear makes you comfortable and gives you confidence, that special "You Factor" will never go out of style.

To give you the most accurate information on men's wear, I consulted with certified image consultant Brian Lipstein, founder and CEO of Henry A. Davidsen, a custom clothing firm based in Philadelphia, who graciously shared his time and the following tips with me.

SUIT YOURSELF

First and foremost, Lipstein states that it pays to buy the best suits you can afford, as a good fitting, well-designed suit makes a visual statement about you each time you wear it. There are three major styles or silhouettes, traditionally named for the countries in which they originated, though it is now quite common to find all three styles in any country.

British: This type of suit is typified by soft, unpadded shoulders and a long, hourglass body with a higher armhole and is either double or single breasted, with two or three buttons and side vents. This jacket shape is designed to follow the body and move with the individual.

Italian or Continental: This cut is epitomized by a light-weight construction, squared shoulders that slant back into the wearer's body, and a short, close-fitting, single-breasted body, with two buttons and a ventless back to emphasize a slim look. This suit was popularized on Wall Street and is often considered the business power suit. If you have a bulkier frame, you should probably avoid this style of suit.

American: This is a natural-shoulder suit with a straight and somewhat roomier body, three buttons, and a center back vent. The popular menswear retailer Brooks Brothers is credited with popularizing the "sack suit" out of the need to fit all body types. The modern version of this style is now a little more tailored, but it is still designed to fit the masses and is the least flattering of the three suit designs. Since this cut is intended to accommodate all body types, it rarely fits anyone extremely well.

A Stitch in Time

The construction of a garment plays the largest role in determining the price of a man's suit. Did you know that lower-end suits are mostly glued together while higher-end suits are sewn together by hand? Keeping this industrial secret in mind, let's explore the options you have for making a suit purchase:

· **An off-the-rack suit**, your least expensive option, is made to a "stock size," or average specification, meaning that nearly everyone who purchases this type of suit will need some tailoring. Unfortunately, many men either aren't aware of the difference tailoring can make or don't care. While alterations improve the fit of an off-the-rack suit, it will rarely hang perfectly. A lower-end line of clothing will vary in price depending on the fabric and construction quality, but the old adage "you get what you pay for" certainly applies.

· **A made-to-measure suit** represents the first level of customization. After you choose the fabric and select a style, the garment is fitted to your measurements. The tailor starts with a preset stock pattern (for example, a size 42 jacket), then adjusts the measurements to the wearer's body *before* the fabric is cut. The result is a much better fit than that of an off-the-rack suit, and you have the option of choosing a higher-quality fabric.

· **A custom-made or *bespoke* men's suit** is the ultimate in luxury because it is constructed entirely by hand. A bespoke suit is more flattering than a made-to-measure suit because the tailor creates a customized pattern based on the client's measurements and proportions. Of course, a custom suit is more costly than the other two options, but well worth it if you desire an impeccable fit, utmost quality, and a longer wearing life.

The Double-Breasted Suit

A two- or three-button suit is great for everyday wear, but there is no comparison to the swagger of a double-breasted suit. This is the perfect suit to wear to important business meetings or lunch with conservative clients and power brokers. When you wear this suit design, be sure to keep all of the buttons buttoned.

Like the classic three-button single-breasted suit, a double-breasted suit looks best on a man of medium or tall build; however, any man can wear the double-breasted, provided the jacket is tailored at the waist. Bringing in the waistline makes the wearer's shoulders become more prominent, drawing the observer's eyes upward and away from the middle. Even if your waistline is wider than your shoulder width, the overlapping lapels on your suit can draw the eye away from your torso.

To Vent or Not to Vent

When shopping for a suit, always pay attention to the back vents, because this often-overlooked design aspect can either help or hurt your appearance. Vents are also an indication of how dressy a suit is. There are three basic styles of vents, and each has both practical and fashion considerations:

· **A center vent** is typically found on more casual blazers or suits. It's the common American cut that is both classic and conservative, but some style experts caution that it offers little or no benefit to your physique. A jacket with a center vent is often shapeless and is typical of off-the-rack suits. If the vent doesn't stay closed when you wear the suit, it doesn't fit properly. Hint: You can often tell a newbie suit wearer because he forgets to cut the threads from the center vent after purchasing the jacket. Try not to make this mistake.

· **Side vents or double vents** are more functional than center vents and offer many benefits. If you have a little extra girth around the midsection, opt for side vents, as the two vertical lines in the back are slimming. Side vents also allow the back of the suit to lie flat, regardless of body type, while offering a greater range of motion.

· **A ventless jacket** provides a clean, slimming appearance but also limits your range of motion. If restricted movement isn't a concern for you, a ventless jacket offers a slimming look even if you're on the hefty side, but keep in mind that proper fit is essential for a trim, polished look.

Pushing Buttons

In my Dress for Success seminars, men often ask if they should button up their jackets whenever they stand up, and the answer is "yes." The jacket should button comfortably without pulling in front (which, unfortunately, can make a stout man appear as if he's wearing a sausage casing), but when the jacket is a good fit, the look adds polish and panache. Regardless of whether you're wearing a two- or three-button suit, remember to leave the bottom button unbuttoned.

Shirt Tales

At one time a shirt may merely have served as the backdrop for a tie, but today shirts have become the focal point. Your choice of shirt is now a way to express your personality and creativity. White, light blue, and pale pink (yes, *pink*) oxford shirts are staples these days, particularly in today's business casual climate, because some men have ditched wearing ties altogether. If you go tieless, your shirt can provide that missing element of color and be the one mode of self-expression that doesn't compromise your professionalism.

Collars: Choose a collar that complements the shape of your face. If you're tall or thin and have an angular or narrow face, it's best to look for a "spread" collar, one that's low and wide. Avoid a straight collar, because it will accentuate the angle of your face and make it appear longer or thinner.

If you have a round face or short neck, choose a straight collar, meaning one that's long and vertically pointed. The vertical point will visually lengthen your facial contours. If your face is an oval shape, most types of medium-length straight or spread collars will work well to balance your face.

Cuffs: A French cuff, also called a double cuff, is always secured with cuff links rather than worn open, folded up, or loose. These cuffs lack button closures, which sets them apart from your average dress shirts. French cuffs are often considered more formal and dressy than buttoned cuffs, yet they are appropriate for daily wear in many professional settings. For a more polished look, try double-sided cuff links such as the handcrafted sets by designer Robin Rotenier (www.Rotenier.com). Whether you choose gold or silver cuff links, always match them to your belt buckle and watch.

If you don't want to spend the extra time fiddling with cuff links, then button cuffs, also called barrel cuffs, are your best option. Button cuffs are most commonly found on ready-made shirts and have buttonholes on one side and buttons on the other.

TIE ONE ON

For years, men have often expressed their personality and individuality in their choice of neckwear. If you wear ties to work, invest in ones made of high-quality silk rather than polyester. And be sure that your tie complements, rather than clashes with, your shirt. If you happen to be color-blind, work with a trusted friend who will help you set up a system for color coding so you don't end up with an odd or embarrassing color clash.

Your tie should not be too long or too short. Instead, it should reach somewhere between the top and middle of your belt buckle. To add sophistication and depth, a lot of men prefer to make a dimple or inverted pleat, just below the knot. The French call this a *cuillère,* which means "spoon" or "scoop."

Bow Ties: Although few men choose to wear them these days, bow ties truly convey a sense of individualism and make a statement about the wearer's personality. Once associated with the nerdy, pocket-protector crowd, today a bow tie can be a symbol of intelligence, charm, and a good sense of humor; all you need is the confidence to pull it off. Check out Edward Armah's gorgeous collection of handmade, one-of-a-kind bow ties at www.edward armah.com.

Go Overboard with Undershirts

Many style experts believe that undershirts are a must when wearing a dress shirt, as they provide a smoother look (especially those made with a little bit of stretch) and protect the shirt from showing signs of perspiration. Your shirt will last longer and require fewer cleanings if you wear an undershirt beneath it. The prospect of lower maintenance and a longer wearing life is a plus, especially if you spend a lot of money on your dress shirts. If you wear your collar open, wear a proper V-neck undershirt instead of a crew-neck style.

It's Wise to Accessorize

Pocket Squares and Collar Pins: Just as Fred Astaire touted the finishing touches for a polished appearance, remember that the little details make a big difference. There are two accessories that add a touch of class to any outfit: a pocket square and a collar pin. You may at first feel a bit overdressed in this casual, minimalist era if you sport a pocket square or a collar pin, but if you want to stand out or have someone notice you, give one or both of these accessories a try and see if you receive any compliments.

Wallet: Do you suffer from "thick-wallet" syndrome? If so, it's probably time to put a hold on your bulging billfold. All you really need to carry is one credit or debit card, your driver's license or ID, and some cash in case you find yourself in a pinch.

You may not be aware of the potential back problems that result from constantly carrying an overstuffed wallet in your back pocket. It's also possible that you don't need an extra bulge in that particular spot, anyway.

My advice is to stop using your wallet as a filing cabinet. Clean out all those old receipts, scrunched-up photos, and member or reward cards and invest in a new, sleek, and more sophisticated wallet by a fine leather goods company such as Tumi, Coach, Bosca, or Montblanc. Or better yet, consider a money clip, which will fit comfortably inside your jacket pocket; it's an elegant and efficient solution for the man who doesn't always wear a jacket.

In addition to streamlining your wallet, make it a habit to get rid of loose change whenever possible, particularly if you have a tendency to play an impromptu chorus of "Jingle Bells" any time you put your hand in your pocket. Leave those coins in your car for use at tollbooths and parking meters or drop some in the tip jar when you visit a coffee or pastry shop.

Tips on How to Choose Shoes

Invest in at least four pairs of high-quality shoes—one pair in dark brown, one pair in oxblood, and two pairs in black leather—because it's best not to wear the same pair of shoes two days in a row. A shoe with clean lines and a classic look will keep you well covered from your professional interactions to a more personal venue. Depending on your personal style, choose either wingtip or cap-toe oxfords with a slight brogue effect (perforated with small holes). Wingtips feature a toe cap that comes to a point in the center and spreads out toward the sides of the shoes, in a shape that somewhat resembles wings, which is how this style got its name.

When you are shopping for a casual shoe, a loafer will add variety to your wardrobe and be quite useful in the hot summer months. Loafers are perfect for traveling, as they are easy to slide off and on while going through airport security lines.

Pair your black suits with black shoes; gray suits with black or dark brown shoes; brown suits with dark brown shoes; and navy suits with black or oxblood-colored footwear. And remember to coordinate your shoe and belt colors.

A Word About Shoe Trees: Shoe trees are an inexpensive way to keep your shoes in mint condition. They not only fill out the shoe and help the leather maintain its original form; they'll also keep your shoes looking new for a long time. When you take your shoes off at the end of a day, insert the trees while your shoes are still warm and pliable. Cedar shoe trees are best because they absorb moisture and odors, but if you travel quite a bit, plastic shoe trees weigh less and work almost as well. Many people are surprised to learn that a good pair of shoes, when kept polished and stored properly, can last for many years and potentially a lifetime.

SECRETS OF "SOCK"CESS

Socks (called hosiery in finer men's stores) not only provide protection, warmth, and ventilation for your feet, they also provide another style element to your wardrobe. Here's the most important point about socks: **they should match your trousers, not your shoes.**

Dress Socks: Dress socks are usually made from fine fabrics such as silk or wool (or blends of both), though wool is the best investment. Wool socks are more durable, they absorb moisture, and keep your feet drier. Wool also helps prevent foot odor because it moderates temperatures, keeping your feet cool during the summer and warm during the winter. You always want to buy over-the-calf dress socks (the longest length available), because no one likes to see a hairy leg exposed when an unsuspecting businessman sits down or crosses his legs.

Casual Socks: Reserve this style of socks for your personal life when you're wearing chinos, slacks, or jeans. With casual socks you can be more daring with color, pattern, and texture. If you work in a creative career or would just like to add a little pizzazz to your outfit, replace those boring, solid black socks with something more interesting—like a Paul Smith striped sock or an argyle pattern. Choosing a sock with personality is a small yet significant way to showcase a hint of style without looking like you're trying too hard. Experiment with plaids, checks, and dots or any other patterns that call to you. Who knows, you may come up with your own sock signature.

Athletic Socks: Athletic socks should never be worn with a business suit. Enough said.

A "Sock"sessful Shopping Tip: When buying socks, get two or three pairs of the same style and color. If or when a sock goes missing in the laundry black hole, you'll still have others that match.

Saving Room for Grooming

Over the years I've learned that while most men want to look appealing, they don't always put in the time and effort to do so. Grooming is an extremely personal topic, depending on which aspect is being discussed, but it's important for me to say that while everything may appear nicely put together on the outside, it's equally important to maintain what's underneath it all. In other words, good grooming includes more than just shaving or styling your hair. Here are some seldom-discussed grooming points for you to consider.

Scents and Sensibilities: If you regularly wear cologne or aftershave, keep in mind that a scent one person likes might repel another. If you apply cologne or aftershave, be sure to lightly spritz or dab—*never* douse or saturate any part of your body with it. Some men spray their clothes with fragrance, and I'm against that, too. Not only is it "too much of a good thing," but it also can stain or discolor clothing. When it comes to scent, please keep in mind that if anyone can detect your presence before you enter a room or after you walk down a hallway you're wearing too much. If you happen to work in a health-care setting, avoid fragrance altogether, as those you come in contact with may have allergies or environmental sensitivities. Suffice to say, when it comes to scent, less is more.

Facial Moisturizer: Some years ago, men wouldn't dream of touching anything that even hinted of skin care, but those days are long gone. You've seen the plethora of products for men in drugstores and department stores, and I encourage you to use some on a regular basis. A lightweight moisturizer with SPF (sun protection factor) is a must if you want to replenish your skin's water content and receive protection from the elements. A good moisturizer will also help lessen the appearance of any wrinkles, if you have them.

Clean, Groomed Nails: Dirty, uncut nails are a turnoff, and short, stubby nails are equally unattractive. If you bite your nails, stop, because others may judge you unfavorably for this nervous habit. As with skin care and moisturizers, get over any biases or reservations you may have about manicures and even pedicures. They're not just for females anymore. Once you've experienced a manicure or pedicure, you'll know why so many women would rather skip a meal to pay for this little luxury than do without.

Hair You Go

Keep stray hairs trimmed and tidy. We've reached a point where real men cook, raise kids, eat quiche, and willingly attend to their physical selves. If your nose, eyebrow, or ear hairs resemble azalea bushes, it's time to trim the hedges. Use a pair of small grooming scissors or clippers to send those stray hairs into permanent exile.

Care for your facial hair. That five o'clock shadow look only works in ads. Don't let your beard achieve mountain-man proportions, unless of course, you *are* a mountain man and live in the wild. If you insist on sporting a beard, keep it groomed and neatly trimmed. You'll get the closest shave when you trim your beard during or after a shower when the hair is its softest. Be sure to use shaving gel and a clean razor and take short strokes to get the best results.

Befriend your local barber. Instead of ducking into a discount haircutter, cultivate a relationship with a skilled barber and consider it an investment, not a cost. Perhaps you've already discovered that going to a barbershop is a straightforward, no-nonsense experience that offers excellent value for the money. According to my good friend and master barber, Thomas Grant of Kennett Square, Pennsylvania, barbers specialize in the art of grooming men's hair and they can consistently give you a close, conservative or stylish, tapered haircut. Every cut is finished off with a shave around your neck and ears, giving you a clean, pristine look and feel. After your haircut, Grant recommends that you treat yourself to a hot-lather face shave, accompanied by a facial, the ultimate pampering experience. He says with conviction that "you haven't lived until you've experienced the pleasures of a great shave by a master barber."

Tame your body mane. Just as a shrub or cherished bonsai need trimming, there comes a point when a jungle of hair needs to be pruned or cut back. If you haven't already considered it (and there's a legitimate need for doing so), you might want to embrace the idea of "manscaping." That is, if you wear open-collared shirts to work, be diligent about trimming, shaving, or waxing any chest hair that might peek out through the top of your shirt.

STYLE MUST-HAVES

• **Watch:** Are you aware that most people will notice what kind of watch you wear? Your watch is the one accessory that you glance at numerous times during the day. A quality Swiss watch will not only take you from day into evening; it will also stylishly enhance anything you wear and last for many, many years. Choose something with a genuine leather band, or if your budget allows, choose a watch in white or yellow gold or a combination of both.

• **Custom-Made Shirts:** The quality, style, and fit of a shirt can upgrade or undermine the look of any suit. At least once in his life, a man should have a couple of custom-made dress shirts. The unbeatable fit and the attention to detail that go into making a shirt that fits you perfectly are well worth every penny you'll spend. This, too, is an investment, not a cost.

• **Cashmere Sweater:** Cashmere quietly speaks of casual elegance and class. This fine wool makes for a soft and comfy sweater that can be worn day or night, depending on the occasion. Choose from a variety of styles—crew neck, V-neck, turtleneck, cardigan, or half-zip sweaters.

• **Navy Blue Blazer:** This is a must-have for business casual occasions or when you're traveling. The classic navy blue blazer never goes out of style.

• **Black Leather Jacket:** This can be worn on weekends or out to dinner with friends or that special someone. Like other classics, your black leather jacket will go equally well with jeans and dress slacks.

· **Coat:** If you live in, or frequently travel to, a cold climate, invest in a quality overcoat, because it's what people will see when they first meet you. You'll be amazed at how many years a good coat will serve you, so choose a timeless, stylish look such as a button-up wool or cashmere coat in black, gray, navy, or camel.

Remember, every time you wear the appropriate attire to work, an interview, or a special event you send the message that you are someone who does your homework. Think about the way the person you're meeting with may dress. Try to objectively see yourself through the eyes of a stranger; consider what your clothes may broadcast about you. And until you've reached the pinnacle of your success, dress for the position you aspire to hold, not the one you currently have.

1. Teach yourself to be extra detail-oriented by coordinating your leather accessories (wallet, briefcase, watchband) with your belt and shoes. Always match the color of your belt to your shoes.

2. Make sure your pocket square coordinates with, but never matches, your tie.

3. Wear pleated and cuffed pants for a more traditional business look or if you feel the need to camouflage any tummy bulge or need more room in the thigh area. Wear flat-front pants if you are short or want a sleeker, leaner look.

4. Wear patent-leather shoes to black-tie affairs only.

5. A black suit should be reserved for funerals, black-tie events, or nighttime fashion.

(continued)

6. It's best not to wear a button-down collared shirt with a business suit, unless you're going for a more casual look.

7. Keep a clean crease in your dress trousers, not in your jeans.

8. Save your all-cotton chinos or Dockers for the weekend. For work, wear trousers that don't wrinkle easily.

9. Don't wear sneakers, boat shoes, or other sport shoes at the office, even on Casual Friday. And save your gym shoes for the gym.

10. Make friends with the bootblack at the airport or near your office and make it a ritual to get your shoes shined weekly and at the beginning of each business trip.

11. Don't wear socks with sandals, unless you want to look like a tourist.

12. Remember: backpacks are for college students. Use your valise or briefcase for a polished, professional appearance.

13. Refrain from wearing white socks with dress shoes, as that can tarnish your image and be a deal-breaker.

CHAPTER 4

The Well-Dressed Woman

FASHION FADES, STYLE IS ETERNAL.
— Coco Chanel, French fashion designer

When asked to name a famous woman, past or present, who perfectly epitomizes classic beauty, individual style, and magnetic attractiveness, many women think of Audrey Hepburn, Sophia Loren, The Duchess of Cambridge (the former Kate Middleton), or Jacqueline Kennedy Onassis. You and I could add our own favorites to this list, but young or old, current or deceased, all of these women share something in common. It's the presence of a certain je ne sais quoi, an intangible, elusive quality that makes them attractive, memorable, and distinct. They all possess what I call their own personal style.

Personal style is not about the brand of watch on your wrist, the pricey outfit you're wearing, or the designer handbag you carry. Style is something you can't buy. It's knowing what clothes make you look and feel your best and knowing how to put them together. When you have this knowledge or knack, you end up looking more complete and feeling more confident, so your personality and uniqueness can shine through.

One of my favorite icons is the legendary Oscar-winning

actress Grace Kelly. With her subtle energy, elegance, and beauty, she became one of Hollywood's most fascinating and enduring stars. As a young actress, she was known for dressing in conventional, understated daywear (wool skirts and cashmere cardigans), yet there was something about her that made men swoon and women want to emulate her.

Despite her understated appearance, Grace knew how to express her originality and make casting agents take notice. She would wear white gloves to auditions (this was unheard of in the acting world), neutral hose, kitten heels, slim wool skirts, a camel-hair coat, horn-rimmed glasses (she was nearsighted), and less-is-more makeup. In 1960, Grace's personal style paid off, as she topped the International Best Dressed List Hall of Fame.

Whether you're auditioning for a movie, interviewing for a job, or meeting a potential client for the very first time, the way you choose to dress and carry yourself is your visual currency. If you expect your clients or customers to pay money for your service or product, you'll want to look like you're worth every penny and then some. You are your own best business card, and when you suit up and step out into the world each day you are sending a message to the world about who you are and how you want to be perceived. That's why it's essential to foster some creativity and originality, so you can dress your best and make the most of what you have, just as Grace Kelly did.

A stylish woman looks like she's en route to the most marvelous "audition" of her life. And before you start thinking, *But I have no style,* just know that we all have our own style, whether we know it or not. Ask some trusted friends about yours. In the meantime, here are some ways to make the most of your wardrobe and gain the competitive edge with your appearance.

DRESS TO INVEST

I frequently hear clients complain that many of their female employees don't know how to dress appropriately for the business environment, especially in companies that have relaxed dress codes. When I'm hired to come into organizations to teach a Dress for Success seminar, I'm often shocked by how some women (and yes, men, too) dress for work. Frequently I see women dressed in the latest and not so greatest trends. Trendy clothes tend to be hip, cutesy, whimsical, fun, or funky, and they tend to change from season to season. Trends may come and go, but women who are serious about career advancement need to remember that *real* style is both timeless and classic.

I define "classic" as "simple, harmonious, and subtly elegant, with lasting significance and worth." Classic attire doesn't have to be bland, boring, or unimaginative. You can convey taste, quality, personality, and style by adding colorful or distinctive "statement" accessories such as jewelry, a silk scarf, shoes, and a fun handbag to your classic pieces (more to come on this subject). First, let's explore how you build a professional core wardrobe.

There are certain essential items, also known as investment pieces, that every career woman should own. These pieces are the staples of your wardrobe and they can be mixed and matched to create your own signature look. If you work in a creative career such as advertising, fashion, retail, or entertainment, you will have more leeway when it comes to dressing for work. Keep in mind, however, you never want to confuse creative or innovative dress with being sloppy or overly casual.

To compile this list of essential or "anchor" pieces, I consulted with certified image and wardrobe consultants Susan Bigsby in

Palm Beach, Florida, and Lauren Vitalie of Vital Image in Denver, Colorado.

Classic Blazer: Whenever you want to project more competence or authority, wear long sleeves. In other words, when your shoulders and arms are covered you are sending a subliminal message that you are "armed" and ready for business. The stateliest piece of clothing you can own is a classic solid black or navy jacket. Wearing a well-made quality jacket over a dress or with a blouse and skirt will elevate your style and help you project more confidence and proficiency. The less skin you show, the more power you convey and the savvier you appear. Keep a tailored, quality jacket in your office at all times so you can put it on at the last minute in case you're invited to give a presentation, meet a client, or attend an important meeting. Make sure your jacket fits well and complements your body style. Jackets with big shoulder pads are not recommended, as they often make you look like a throwback to the 1980s.

Perfectly Tailored Black Suit: Every professional woman should own at least one classic wool or wool-blend black suit consisting of a skirt, jacket, and pants. Flat-front trousers are more slimming than pleated trousers and can be worn with or without the jacket. The hemline of the trousers should fall between the top of the shoe heel and mid-heel.

A solid-colored A-line or pencil skirt is chic and flattering on most women. In keeping with what has become the classic business length, the bottom of the skirt should reach the top of the knee or the middle (my preference) or just below the knee. Save your mid-calf skirts for more casual occasions and your short or micro-minis (if you have any) for nightclubbing or weekend wear. Find a talented seamstress who can customize or alter your suit so it fits perfectly.

White Fitted Shirt: A crisp, contoured, cotton button-down white shirt always looks fresh and goes with everything. You can easily enhance your own style by adding a big, bold, colorful belt or a fun and funky necklace. Wear it with a nice pair of light wool trousers and a gold or silver chain belt for a smart casual look or pair it with a dark pantsuit and pearls for a more traditional business look. Launder or dry-clean your blouse as necessary to keep the armpits from yellowing so you don't have to retire it prematurely.

Silk or Cashmere Sweater Set: A quality twinset (a simple shell and cardigan) can be more comfortable and less formal than a blouse and blazer, and it's light and easy to pack for business trips. A twinset is also great to wear on business casual days because it offers a softer, more approachable look than a fitted business suit. Choose hues that complement your skin and hair coloring.

Trench Coat: You'll never go wrong with a good-quality coat, especially a double-breasted, belted, traditional trench coat. It can work in any kind of weather and goes with almost everything, from jeans to a business suit. Although solid basic colors like khaki and black are universal and timeless, you could also express your individuality by purchasing a coat that has some flair and color. There's something about a trench that not only attracts attention but also gives you an appearance of refinement. Many years ago when I worked for Northwest Airlines, the female flight attendants wore striking, eye-catching red trench coats and we received many compliments on our signature style.

Little Black Dress (LBD): The right LBD is another significant piece in your wardrobe that never goes out of style, as long as you keep it plain and simple. It's not about buttons, bows, or any kind of excess. Instead, choose a timeless, flattering silhouette and dress it up or down with accessories, depending on the time of day and the occasion. You can wear your little black dress with pearls and pumps to the office and then change into diamonds and stilettos for an evening out on the town.

Accessories

Shoes: Long ago, footwear was an indicator of one's prosperity level. People who could afford to regularly repair or reheel their shoes were considered "well-heeled." Even today, good-looking shoes can help you step up and stand out, so don't hesitate to buy the best shoes you can afford. (Yes, this may be the best news you'll hear all day—buy shoes; buy good ones.) You have a wide selection to choose from, but when shopping for work shoes start with one or two pairs of classic and comfortable basic black leather pumps with a moderate heel. From there you can branch out to more specialized designs. Take your shoes to a reputable shoe repair shop when your heels start to show the first signs of wear and tear.

Hosiery: Unless it's extremely cold outside, most women today prefer not to wear pantyhose. So if you wear skirts or dresses to work, make sure that your legs are tanned and toned. Leg sprays and self-tanners can give your legs a radiant glow, hide many imperfections, and are much safer than the harmful rays of the sun. If you choose to wear pantyhose to work, wear shades that are solid and sophisticated. Sheer nude shades by Donna Karan are great for spring and summer, while black and brown light-weight opaque tights will give you some variety in the fall and winter. Avoid the dated suntan-colored hose. And never wear pantyhose (especially those with a reinforced toe) with open-toe or peep-toe shoes. Style rule: **if you see the toes, wear no hose.** If you like to wear pants to work, choose semi-sheer, calf-length trouser socks or knee-high stockings that match the color of your trousers. Or you can forfeit wearing the socks and knee highs altogether.

Sunglasses: Your eyes are worth protecting, so make sure you own at least one pair of designer shades.

Jewelry: It's important to invest in classic accessories such as simple diamond studs, gold and silver hoop earrings, a quality strand of pearls, and a stately watch. You might also want to buy unique pieces of jewelry that accentuate your signature style to spruce up a simple outfit. Former secretary of state and UN ambassador Madeleine Albright is often seen wearing an eclectic brooch to brighten her business suit; this is her signature statement piece. For work, it's best to avoid bangle bracelets, as they tend to get in the way and make noise when you shake someone's hand. If you feel compelled to wear one, wear it on your left wrist. Long, dangling chandelier earrings, toe rings, and ankle bracelets can also be a distraction, so save those items for after hours. With jewelry, it helps to remember that less is more.

The Silk Scarf: For decades, stylish women have worn silk scarves. Silk is a luxurious and sensuous fabric and has a reputation of being associated with wealth and success. Silk scarves are considered the most popular fashion accessory sold today, and they provide endless possibilities for enhancing your wardrobe. They can be worn as a head covering, a belt, a shawl, or a neckerchief. Scarves add a bit of refinement, elegance, and a splash of color to what might otherwise be a nondescript outfit. Choose one in your signature color to enhance your natural beauty when wearing it near your face.

A Great Handbag: All women should own at least one classic handbag (okay, maybe two or three) that will go anywhere. In choosing a bag, remember, the more structure the bag has, the more formal it is. I recommend:

- **An all-purpose tote bag:** for daytime or carrying all your essentials while you travel. A quality leather or canvas structured tote bag is a great investment, travels well, and will last for years if you take care of it.

- **A clutch or wristlet:** just the right size to carry essentials such as your ID, your driver's license, and lipstick. It also easily slips into a briefcase if you have to go from the office to a networking event. It's small and lightweight and will not get in the way of handshaking, eating, or drinking at social functions.

- **A medium-sized structured handbag, with rolled leather or chain-link straps:** this bag is a bit more formal and should be a staple in your working wardrobe. Purchase one in a neutral color to coordinate with the dominating colors of your most-often-worn work attire, as well as a brightly colored one to give a solid-colored outfit some vim and vigor.

THE BARE ESSENTIALS

Never underestimate the power of the proper undergarments. I wish it weren't true, but the older we get, the more support we need as our body parts head south. Here are some tips to keep in mind when you are shopping for the "bare" necessities.

Shapewear: I'm at the point in my life where I don't feel properly dressed for work if I'm not wearing the most important accessory in my wardrobe—Spanx. Body shapers like those from Spanx.com can mold, shape, minimize, and actually enhance your natural curves, making you look thinner, smoother, tighter, smaller, higher, and sexier. Whether you're wearing a fitted dress or a pair of slacks, shapewear can help you conceal a multitude of sins, visible panty lines, back and belly fat, saddlebags, or a muffin top.

Bra: The right bra is also very important to prevent your parts from puckering, creeping, spilling, or sagging. You've probably seen women who wear clothing that reveals their bra or panty lines, and this is a big faux pas. It's nice to have a variety of bras in different colors and designs, but for your work wardrobe invest in slightly padded, unadorned, fitted bras that match your skin tone or outfit. I cringe whenever I see a woman's high beams poking through her form-fitting blouse or thin jacket or top. When you're in business mode, you'll want to gain and hold attention, but not with any body part below the neck. It's best not to wear a white bra under a black top (and vice versa) and to keep your straps tight enough so they don't slip off your shoulders. If you've never had a formal bra-fitting consultation I recommend one.

JUST FOR FUN

The following items may or may not be appropriate for your workplace or professional position, but they are still great staples to have on hand when you need something to wear in the evening, on weekends, or when you're traveling.

A Knit Top: This is also known as the "all-occasion top." Invest in two or three solid black and solid white tops of varying weights, necklines, and sleeve lengths. Keep in mind that V-necks and quarter-length sleeves are universally the most flattering. Light merino wool and cashmere blends work in every season and are great for layering. Choose a silhouette and color that complement your body type and skin tone.

A Great Pair of Jeans: Dark jeans without ornamentation are dressier and more flattering and will give you the most options. The right pair of jeans can be easily dressed up or down and can be worn with a variety of jackets, shoes, and boots. The most comfortable jeans are those that stretch and move with your body. Choose jeans that aren't too long or too short and that don't hang too low or ride up too high on your hips. When it comes to jeans, a combination of the right fit with the right style is the secret to looking your best.

Black Boots: Stylish and sophisticated, black leather boots in different styles and heel lengths can be worn anywhere with anything, from skirts and dresses to jeans.

A Finishing Touch Can Mean So Much

A Good Hairdresser: Your hair is as much a part of your wardrobe as any piece of clothing. It's one of the most important accessories you (and others) see each and every day. I'm a firm believer that you should change your hairstyle at least once a year to keep you looking fresh and current. If you're still wearing the same hairstyle you had in college or if you're throwing your hair into a ponytail every day, it's time for a new you. The right hairstyle can highlight your best facial features and help you look years younger as you age. If you color your hair, keep it fresh so those telltale roots don't ruin your look.

Kiss and Makeup: When applied correctly, makeup can accentuate your best features and make you appear more radiant, attractive, and energetic. The right type and amount of makeup

will give you a more flawless, polished look, because it can conceal age spots, acne, blemishes, and other imperfections that appear as we age.

To find out what colors and products look best on you, treat
yourself to a makeup lesson at an upscale department store. This
is an economical way to learn a few professional tricks you can
use at home. International makeup artist Andrew C. Petersen
recommends finding someone you trust who will guide you
in what you need for a particular season. "It's beneficial to bring
in some of the products you already own so the makeup artist can
recommend items to complement your collection," says Petersen.
He advises visiting the same makeup artist several times a year
so that you can slowly build a professional relationship with him
or her.

When you put on makeup it's like putting on the right outfit:
when you wear it, you'll look more put together. "When you carve
out time to put on your makeup, no matter how extensive or minimal, you are giving yourself a gift," says Petersen. "As I see it,
beauty shines from within and makeup is your frame."

Maintaining Your Brows: Your makeup might change from
season to season, but the shape of your eyebrows should always
stay the same. The brows are your most important, yet under-
appreciated, feature on your face. They're seen every time someone looks into your eyes. For a more polished look, get them
professionally trimmed and shaped on a regular basis. It's like
getting a facelift without the surgery.

My Two Cents About Scents: If your fragrance enters the
room before you do or lingers in the room long after you have left,
it's too strong. Like all good things, perfume should be used in
moderation, especially at work, where others may be allergic to
fragrance. Play it safe—wear a lightly fragranced body lotion to work

instead of perfume. On special occasions or evenings out on the town, perfume can make you feel pretty and even sexy. Apply it *before* you get dressed so you don't stain your clothes or jewelry.

Teeth: The first thing most people notice about us is our smile. If your teeth are crooked, stained, dark, dingy, yellow, or missing, they can ruin your entire appearance. In a recent Harris Interactive Poll, 94 percent of adults said that they are likely to notice a person's smile the first time they meet someone. Eighty-five percent thought that a person's smile was "very or somewhat important" on a first meeting. Your smile is a crucial part of your personality and can affect your self-esteem. If you're not happy with your smile or feel embarrassed or self-conscious about the appearance of your teeth, consult with a cosmetic dentist and find out how you can turn your frown upside down. When you have an attractive smile, it can enhance your appearance and boost your confidence, both personally and professionally.

Nails: Another detail that most people (especially men) notice is a woman's nails. Long, dragon-lady nails are as unprofessional as short, chewed-up nails. Try not to ever leave for work with chipped nail polish. Keep your fingernails neat, clean, and painted in a clear, sheer or solid, professional color. Nail art is great for special occasions but not for the workplace. If you wear sandals or other open-toe shoes, keep your feet in good condition and your toes perfectly polished.

DRESS WITH FINESSE

Here are some final tips to keep in mind if you want to consistently maintain a professional appearance, be taken seriously, and get ahead in the workplace.

Avoid "mood" dressing. Whenever you feel less than your best, take extra care in choosing an outfit that will enhance your mood, not announce it. Granted, we all have those days when we don't feel particularly energetic or motivated. This is when we're most tempted to gravitate toward comfort clothes to match our mood. Have you ever been tempted to grab the most drab, loose-fitting outfit in your closet, usually something dark or somber looking and not the least bit flattering? The message, whether we know it or not, is probably some variation of "just let me hide inside myself today" or "please don't look at me or speak to me." For some reason, we women are sometimes prone to communicating from the inside out. Well, I'm a proponent of communicating from the outside in; that is, it's very important to try to look your best, *especially* when you're feeling wiped out, unmotivated, or bloated. Wearing comfort clothes to work will only bring you down and keep you there. Dress "up" and choose flattering colors and lines that will raise your spirits and inspire you to be in a better mood.

Sexy equals self-sabotage. There is nothing positive to be gained whenever you expose your cleavage, even a little bit, or wear ultra-short skirts or snug, form-fitting clothes. Yes, you may attract wandering eyes, but showcasing your body parts can be your undoing. Don't be like those women who let their abilities and intellect get overshadowed by a certain "look," diminishing their chances for a job opportunity or a promotion.

According to Peter Glick, a psychology professor at Lawrence University in Appleton, Wisconsin, "Although physical attractiveness is generally an advantage in the workplace, a sexy self-presentation harms businesswomen who are in, or who aspire to, managerial jobs." In short, if you want to get ahead in the workplace and be taken seriously, dial down your sex appeal so your capabilities and competence shine through.

Think before you ink. The face and body of today's entry-level employee is changing, and they're increasingly decorated with body art and jewelry parts. In workplaces such as graphic design firms, salons, and retailers targeting the younger set, piercings and tattoos may be acceptable and even considered assets. But in traditional, more conservative industries, it's best to cover the tats and remove the studs before you show up at work.

A Quest for the Best

Now that I've guided you through my style strategies, you're ready to take off and find your own signature style. I hope that I've given you some handy tools to discover your best features and favorite wardrobe pieces. Learning to make the most of your wardrobe is a huge element of personal style. Many of the world's most well-dressed women know that personal style entails knowing yourself, investing in your appearance, and allowing the natural light of your personality to shine through, from the inside to the outside. You can do the same, on your own terms and in your own way.

CHAPTER 5

Sound Advice

**YOUR TONE OF VOICE OFTEN SAYS MORE ABOUT WHAT
IS IN YOUR MIND THAN YOUR WORDS DO.**
— NAPOLEON HILL, BESTSELLING AUTHOR

If the first thing people notice about us is our appearance, the
next notable impression is how we sound. Your voice, your unique
way of expressing yourself, is the second thing people notice,
and regardless of how you sound when you speak, you can
strengthen your voice and make it more powerful. Sound is sen-
sation, language is power, and diction is destiny.

Every time we open our mouths, we tell people a lot about
who we are. If you've ever thought that TV hosts and commenta-
tors sound suspiciously similar, you're right, but they didn't
start out that way. Many of them had to alter their accents. One of
my college professors told me that I would never make it in
broadcasting because of my Southern accent. Imagine what that
did to my self-esteem. Now I know better.

There's hope for all of us; even if your voice tends toward
being high-pitched or sharp, you can modify it toward a more
pleasant timbre. Similarly, if you have a nasal twang, a strong

regional accent, or an inclination toward speaking in mono-tone, you can improve how you sound. Some of us have embar-rassing laughs or unusual speech patterns, and these distracting mannerisms can hold us back from promotions or career ad-vancement.

It may seem odd, but all of who you are as a person, every-thing that comprises "you," is considered your "brand." Quirky mannerisms and speech patterns can have a negative effect on your brand, and they could potentially thwart your plans to scale the ladder of success.

Here are four areas in which you can improve your verbal patterns:

- Pronunciation or accent

- Vocabulary

- Voice tone

- Sentence structure

Speak for Yourself

You can improve your speech and fortify your brand with the help of CDs or a speech coach. The coach can teach you how to make some very simple, small adjustments in your manner of speech that will have a profound effect on the way you come across to others. Start listening more closely to yourself and others. Com-pare your speaking patterns to some of your colleagues, clients, or leaders you respect. In the meantime, here are some tips to improve your vocabulary and speech patterns:

• Avoid "skid" talking. That's when a person occasionally drops their *g*s. For example, if you say "goin'" instead of "going," that's skid talking. Often in casual situations some of us tend to run our words together, such as saying "I'm unnago" instead of "I'm going to go."

• Eliminate filler words, including "like," "you know," "umm," and "ah." These words fill in space while you try to think of something to say next. You're better off being silent than using filler words. They can give the impression that you're hesitant to express yourself or you're not sure what you're talking about.

• Add authority to what you say by lowering your voice a notch. If you are giving a presentation and need extra volume, resist the tendency to raise your pitch. Drop your tone slightly to raise your volume.

• Record yourself talking to friends with your smart phone or digital recorder and play it back when you're alone. You may be surprised by what you hear, but once you get over the shock of what you sound like to others try to objectively evaluate your strengths and areas for improvement.

The most accurate indicator of your social stature is not your accent (thank goodness, since I still have a slight Southern accent) but your vocabulary. Grammar and word usage can create a great linguistic divide between social levels, so avoid using double negatives: "I barely got no sleep last night" or "I don't need none."

When you reach a certain level in your career, colleagues, clients, and prospects will be mindful of the words you choose, the way you pronounce them, and your sentence structure.

The good news is it's fairly easy to develop a more extensive vocabulary. All you need is time, patience, and the willingness to read as much as possible. Most bookstores and libraries carry books and CDs on building a more powerful vocabulary, and you can also find some great resources online. My mother, who only had a high school diploma, would read the newspaper from cover to cover every day as a way to expand her vocabulary.

In addition to vocabulary size, grammar is also an indicator of our background. Here are some common bloopers you may have heard, or perhaps there was a time you used a couple of these examples yourself:

- "Him and me went to the store."

- "Please join Bob and I at our table."

- "Irregardless of the situation, I'm still not convinced."

- "Where is she at?"

- "I have went to that restaurant a few times."

- "She ain't here right now."

- "I seen that movie last night."

We may not realize that we are often judged by our sentence structure. In John T. Molloy's *New Women's Dress for Success*, he writes: "A professor of mine once said you can tell a person's background simply by asking if she (or he) would like ice cream on a hot day. If she says, 'Yeah,' she is lower class; if she says, 'Yes,' she is middle class; if she says, 'Yes, I would, thank you,' she is upper class." Molloy says his professor based his statement on the fact that people from poor backgrounds are largely nonverbal and people from upper-class backgrounds tend to speak in complete sentences and are usually taught to be very polite.

Molloy goes on to say that if you make a conscious effort to speak in complete sentences or phrases and to be courteous and polite, you will "appear more sophisticated, intelligent, capable, and attractive."

The amount of money you make has nothing to do with the way in which you speak. In other words, you can be the wealthiest man or woman in town, but no one will know that if your grammar skills are flawed or your pronunciation leaves a lot to be desired. My friend Marilyn Murray Willison equates this to being able to afford a brand-new car yet not knowing how to drive it.

Develop a more confident-sounding voice and you'll find that others will automatically have more confidence in you. Just as it doesn't take a miracle makeover to enhance your physical image, you can do the same with your oral self-expression. With a little bit of work you can modulate your tone, refine your diction, and upgrade your grammar and word usage, and everything you say will sound more eloquent and interesting.

CHAPTER 6

Discover and Create Your Personal Brand

IF YOU'RE ABLE TO BE YOURSELF, THEN YOU HAVE NO COMPETITION. ALL YOU HAVE TO DO IS GET CLOSER AND CLOSER TO THAT ESSENCE.

— BARBARA COOK, SINGER AND TONY AWARD—
WINNING ACTRESS

Whether we know it or not, each and every one of us has his or her own brand. By definition, personal branding is the process by which we "market" ourselves to others. Every day, all of us have the opportunity to sell ourselves in various professional capacities, from trying to impress our managers so we can take on bigger projects to persuading clients that we have the solution to their current problems or convincing our significant other to try a new restaurant.

From your outward appearance, to what your business card looks like, to what you post on Facebook and other social media sites, everything (and I do mean *everything*) is tied to your personal brand.

Personal branding is not limited to celebrities like Donald

Trump, Kim Kardashian, Oprah Winfrey, Rachael Ray, or Michael Jordan. Management guru and bestselling author Tom Peters was right when he said, "Regardless of age, regardless of position, regardless of the business we happen to be in, we all need to understand the importance of branding. We are CEOs of our own companies: Me, Inc." You are your own "Me, Inc.," and what you wear and how you behave in every venue is part of your personal brand.

Yes, brands can happen by accident, but I certainly don't recommend that method; it leaves too much to chance. I suggest that you discover and carefully cultivate your brand if you are set on enjoying a successful career. Whether you're a job seeker, consultant, student, employee, or entrepreneur, your personal brand is what people will remember about you. It's your image, your reputation, your credibility.

How Your Brand Distinguishes You

Has anyone ever described you as being intelligent, charming, or humorous? If so, that quality is part of your brand, especially if you feel that it accurately characterizes you. You know you have a truly successful brand when your contacts think of you first when they hear a certain phrase, concept, or occupation. For example, when my friends and clients hear the words "manners" and "etiquette," they immediately think of me. This didn't happen by accident.

Being an etiquette expert is more than an occupation to me; it's also a way of life. It's important to me that I not only "practice what I preach but also preach what I practice." Etiquette is the hinge pin of my brand.

It helps to remember that your brand exists whether you create it or not. Again, I say, why leave things to chance? To discover, develop, and deliver your brand, remember this equation:

YOUR SELF-IMPRESSION $+$ HOW PEOPLE PERCEIVE YOU
$$= YOUR\ BRAND$$

You now know that if you don't purposefully brand yourself, someone else will brand you. Granted, how others perceive your brand and what they say about your brand are as powerful as what you say about yourself. Spend some time writing down the kind of comments or feedback you've received from clients, coworkers, your boss, and others. Consider how you feel about this list. Next, ask yourself, "What do I want to be known for?" Then select a niche so that you can position yourself in the marketplace. Once you figure this out and have a solid list of self-impressions and how others perceive you, it's time to create your brand.

The Brand Called You

As the chief marketing officer of Me, Inc., always think of yourself as that one-of-a-kind brand called You. According to Dan Schawbel, the leading personal branding expert for Gen Y and the author of *Me 2.0*, everyone should have a personal branding tool kit. This may consist of one or more of the following: a blog, Web site, business card, résumé, video résumé, portfolio, or social network profiles. Schawbel believes that "your brand must be consistent and reinforce each part of your toolkit."

There are other items that belong in your branding tool kit, including some obvious things that many of us take for granted or completely forget about:

Your Car: You might think of your vehicle as simply a means to get you from point A to point B, but in reality your car (like everything else) says a lot about who you are and how you package yourself. Your car needs more than just fuel and routine maintenance—it needs to be kept clean and neat, both inside and out. You never know when a client might suggest taking your car to lunch because his or her car is in the shop. If your car is dirty or cluttered, it sends a message that you're sloppy and disorganized. But there's another hidden motive as to why a client may ask you to drive.

Did you know that your car may reveal parts of your character? Dr. Leon James at the University of Hawaii (who has researched and taught *the psychology of driving*) claims that your vehicle choice says a lot about your attitude and personality. Whether your car is racy, luxurious, or practical, it makes a statement about you. "People seek attributes in their automobiles that mirror their self-image," says James. A dented, dirty, messy, or poorly functioning vehicle could indicate a neglectful attitude, among other things.

If you're a smoker, never smoke in your car, because nonsmokers will be able to smell the odor on your clothes as well as your breath. Always carry breath mints with you, and pop one or two in your mouth before you meet with clients or customers. This is a good practice, even if you don't smoke.

Your Résumé or Portfolio: It's a job-search jungle out there, and if you're on the hunt for a new position, you'll need every advantage you can get. Barry Shiflett, career management services director at Florida International University's College of

Business Administration, says that the average time a recruiter or company official spends scanning a résumé is only thirteen seconds. At a career fair, the number goes down to eight seconds.

Combine that reality with the high unemployment rate and job seekers have their work cut out for them. Try to think of your written or visual support material (résumé, portfolio, or brochure) as if it were part of a big ad campaign. Every piece of documentation you bring to an interview is every bit as important as what you wear and what you say.

"The sole purpose of a résumé is to get an interview," says Shiflett. "Make every word count." Recruiters and managers often see résumés that are too general and not targeted to a particular position. They also see plenty of typos, misspellings, vague information, and résumés that miss details such as dates. Take a hard look at your résumé and improve or update it every six months even if you are currently happily, gainfully employed.

Remember that everything you say, do, or wear represents your brand. Whenever you go on job interviews or visit clients or prospects, carry your résumé, notepad, or promotional materials in a quality binder or briefcase. You will also receive bonus points by carrying a good-looking and functional pen. These accessories will complete your appearance, add status, and (if you take good care of them) last for many years.

Stationery and Business Cards: It doesn't matter if you're a college student, CEO, or consultant, you should have your own business card. With today's technology, it's easy and inexpensive to create your own, or better yet, you can order a box of cards from an office supply store or printing company. Your business card should contain your personal brand statement, such as "licensed air-conditioning specialist," as well as your contact information and corporate logo, if you have one.

Business cards are an important part of your business wardrobe. I favor business cards printed on heavy stock (at least 90 lb.). Choose a color that best reflects your brand. Ecru (also known as buff, cream, ivory, or eggshell) and white are the most popular, but gray, blue, pink, yellow, and other colors are also available if you want to be a bit more flamboyant or express your less serious side. If you are not yet employed (or are in between jobs), invest in a calling card. It's almost the same thing as a business card except it contains only your name and contact information.

In the business world, courtesy counts and personal thank-you notes are making a comeback. Show your gratitude to clients and prospects with a card or handwritten note that matches the impression you want to make. Every executive should own his or her own personalized, engraved thank-you notes or correspondence cards, made from 100 percent cotton paper. Noticeably soft to the touch, cotton-fiber papers look brighter and crisper than wood-pulp papers, and printed colors appear richer on their surface. The simple elegance of cotton papers, like those sold at Crane & Co. (Crane.com), broadcasts quality and credibility.

Engraved stationery is more expensive than thermographed or lithographed stationery, but the look and feel are well worth it. Again, choose a color and design that best reflects your business and your brand. Keep your stationery in a special desk drawer so it's handy to reach when you want to send off a quick note.

Your Work Space: Whether it's a cubicle, a private office that overlooks a cityscape, or a spare room in your home, your work environment is a part of the package that tells people who you are. For many of us, a desk is much more than just a place to sit and work. It's where we spend a good share of our waking hours, and sometimes it's a little scary to think that we might spend more time working at our desks than sleeping in our own beds.

From an open environment, to a cubicle, to a private office, your work space showcases a wealth of telltale information to your coworkers, bosses, and clients, so it's important for you to evaluate your area with a critical eye.

On the one hand, if your desk is littered with piles of files, loose paper, or sticky notes or is surrounded by stacks of magazines, wads of candy wrappers, or empty soda cans, you are in need of a makeover. Conversely, a work space that is completely barren and void of any personal items says something, too. If your office or work space is a reflection of your brand, what do you want it to say about you?

Unless your company has strict guidelines for decorating your work space, don't be afraid to demonstrate to your colleagues and clients that you have a life; just keep it neat, organized, and interesting. You may want to display a well-framed photograph on your desk, a souvenir from your travels on your bookcase, and a decorative lamp or other office artifacts that reflect who you are. If clients visit your office regularly or if you're in a high-traffic area, err on the conservative side—others may find your collection of sports team mugs or teddy bears tiresome rather than tasteful.

Your Photograph: If you're still using the same professional photograph you used back in college, it's time for another photo shoot. A well-done current photograph is an important part of your professional packaging because it can be used on your business cards, Web site or blog, and social networking sites. If you're ever featured in a magazine or newspaper or asked to speak at a conference, you may well be asked for a photograph and you'll need to have one on hand that you can e-mail in an instant.

Hire a professional photographer instead of asking your brother or favorite uncle to take a shot with his digital camera. If you're a woman, go the extra mile and hire a professional to style your hair and apply flattering makeup for a flawless appearance.

Select the outfit that best represents you, something slightly conservative that won't go out of style in a couple of years. Make sure it hangs nicely whether you're standing or sitting. Wear a solid color that flatters your hair color and complexion. Choose a look that appropriately fits your corporate culture and your personal brand, as well as your clientele and marketplace. Save the glamorous, rugged, or dramatic looks for personal use. Your photograph, like your brand, should mirror your professionalism and credibility.

PART TWO

POLISH

CHAPTER 7

Networking Not Working? Foster Friendships Instead

WISHING TO BE FRIENDS IS QUICK WORK, BUT FRIENDSHIP IS A SLOW-RIPENING FRUIT.

— ARISTOTLE, GREEK PHILOSOPHER AND TEACHER

Vincent van Gogh once said, "There is nothing more truly artistic than to love people." Although I love people (most of them anyway), I didn't always love networking with people...until a few years ago. We're all familiar with the concept of networking, and there are some myths about this social practice that I'd like to clear up. First of all, there's an assumption that you have to be "good" at networking or it won't get you anywhere. And we're often told that while it's important to know a lot of people, I agree with my wise and witty Granny Johnson, who always said, "It's not who you know; it's who knows you."

Networking is *not* a numbers game; it's not about how many business cards you pass out or collect. It's not about how many products you can sell or whom you can instantly impress, exploit, or schmooze to get what you want. Proper networking is a gradual process of making genuine connections with people and cultivating those relationships for the long term.

I'm sure you've seen people at networking events who appear almost predatory, approaching their targets as if stalking prey. And just like in the animal kingdom, when human beings sense that they are being hunted they flee for their lives. The most crucial aspect of networking is how you and the other person connect for the first time.

If people try to foist their wares or wants on us without first establishing a relationship, we either hang up on them, refuse to return their phone calls, avoid them at social gatherings, delete their e-mails, or disregard their requests to connect on social networking sites. To put it bluntly, an exploitive mentality is completely ineffective and self-defeating when you're trying to establish a relationship with someone who doesn't know you.

The most effective networking takes place when you are willing to tithe your social capital. In other words, look for opportunities to be *of service* to others instead of thinking about how they can meet your needs. I'm suggesting that you train your ears to hear a problem so you can present a solution.

For example, if a work colleague mentions that she needs a good mechanic, you might not know one, but someone in your network probably does. Send an e-mail, make a phone call, do a little research, and when someone gives you the name of a trusted mechanic pass it along to your colleague. She will be forever grateful for your kind and unsolicited efforts.

Here are some additional ways to manifest your social capital, expand your sphere of influence, and form solid, mutually beneficial business relationships.

Why Be Shy?

If you've ever felt shy in social situations, you're not alone. According to Bernardo J. Carducci, Ph.D., author of *Shyness: A Bold New Approach* and the director of the Shyness Research Institute at Indiana University Southeast, almost 95 percent of us know firsthand what it means to be shy in some situations. "Shyness does not equal low self-esteem," says Dr. Carducci. "It's not a disease, personality deficit, or character flaw." The good news is that you can be shy and still be sociable.

Instead of spending small amounts of time with a lot of people, I suggest spending more time with a smaller number of carefully chosen people. You may find it comforting to know that the strength and longevity of your relationships depend more on the *quality* and far less upon the quantity of your connections.

Try not to allow your fears to inhibit you from interacting with others. Understand that you have more to contribute than you think. If you never make the effort, you'll cut yourself off from potential opportunities as well as deprive others of your unique gifts. Speak to strangers now and practice introducing yourself in low-threat situations so that when opportunities present themselves you'll be more comfortable interacting with people you don't know.

Enjoy the Depth and Breadth of Diversity

It's natural to gravitate toward people who are just like us, but did you know that you do yourself a disservice when you socialize with the same people all the time? When I attend conferences or networking events, I usually see people engage in a behavior I call clustering. This is when people who know one another get into groups, either sitting or standing, while they pretty much ignore everyone else around them. Clustering seems to be a natural tendency, but why hang out with those you know or see every day when there are so many new possibilities in the room?

Maybe our clustering behavior is a carryover from childhood, when we were warned not to talk to strangers; however, staying in familiar territory defeats the purpose of networking and connecting. How else will you broaden your horizons? At least once per social event, deliberately choose to interact with someone you don't know or would not normally be drawn to. If you're willing to break out of your comfort zone (or at least stretch it) and initiate a conversation with someone new, you just might learn something new or satisfy your curiosity quotient.

Did you know that having a sense of curiosity has been linked to happiness? In his book, *Curious?: Discover the Missing Ingredient to a Fulfilling Life,* Todd Kashdan, a psychology professor from George Mason University, tells readers that curious people have a higher level of well-being. When we take the initiative to try something new, our brain produces the chemical dopamine, which kicks in whenever we're in a safe yet unfamiliar situation. Higher levels of dopamine can elevate a person's spirits, so if you want to feel better, let your curiosity come out. Instead of gravitating toward the predictable and familiar, go in the other direction and unleash your curiosity. Increased levels of dopamine generate a feeling of well-being and put us in high spirits.

How fun it is to discover there are benefits to having an inquiring mind. In fact, this is part of what separates the extraordinary individuals from the ordinary ones. Just as our body must have oxygen, our brain both craves and benefits from stimulation in the form of new experiences, new activities, and new people. It's what separates the commonplace from the uncommon.

For every social event you attend, I encourage you to seek diversity in your connections. Introduce yourself to someone who appears most unlike you, or someone you might otherwise avoid or overlook. Find out what you can about this person. Then as you become more adventurous, spend time with people from as many different professions or cultural and social groups as possible. In time, you'll discover that having diverse relationships will bring you new ideas, fresh perspectives, and a broader range of opportunities.

DEVELOP CONVERSATIONAL CURRENCY

When you meet new people, take time to establish rapport. The most common mistake most executives make is that of lapsing into business talk too soon, so take time to form a connection that has some substance. And the best way to do this is by telling your story or by trying to get others to reveal their stories (and everyone has a story to tell).

Stories are the most basic tool for connecting us to one another. Research shows that storytelling not only engages all the senses; it also triggers activity on both the left and the right sides of the brain. People attend, remember, and are transformed by stories. Many of us grew up listening to stories passed from generation to generation by our parents or grandparents. Even in the world of business, stories have a unique power to move people's hearts, minds, feet, and wallets in the storyteller's intended direction.

One way to discover a person's story is by asking the right questions. Some of my favorite questions include: "If you weren't in this line of work, what would you like to do?" and "Whom do you most admire?" Most people enjoy talking about themselves, and these kinds of questions make people open up. In no time they often reveal their background, motivations, philosophy, and challenges. In the process, you can learn a lot if you allow it. The best part about listening to someone's story is that you gain respect by simply sharing your time, listening and responding with warm intent, and making a genuine effort to understand his or her world. You don't have to agree with everything the person says; all you have to do is be fully present and engaging.

In many of my seminars, we do an exercise called Getting to Know You. I ask all attendees to partner with someone in the room whom they barely know or don't know at all. I instruct them to sit face-to-face, and then I say, "Think of a special person in your life who influenced who you are today, and then tell your partner who that person is and how they inspired you." As one person shares, the other is instructed to listen, and then I ask them to switch roles.

After approximately seven minutes, I stop the exercise. I'm always amazed to learn that most of the "share pairs" have either something in common or stories that end up being somewhat similar.

After doing this exercise with numerous groups, I'm still intrigued by the fact that the same results happen time and time again. This exercise oftentimes brings out a person's authenticity and vulnerabilities. When you share a part of your true self with someone, the other person is more inclined to share information about themselves, too, which brings about a connection that often leads to a new friendship.

In short, if you want to better understand a client, a colleague, or anyone else, you have to connect at a level beyond the superficial. This means that you must be willing to talk about subjects more meaningful than the weather, traffic, or celebrity gossip (unless of course, one of those subjects profoundly affects your livelihood).

Being open and asking for openness in return works in your favor when done in moderation. Be selective as to where, when, and with whom to share personal information, because not everyone will be sensitive to your situation or respect your privacy. However, if you're discerning and expose your more vulnerable side in a tasteful and prudent manner to the right individual at the right time, he or she will likely identify, empathize, and think, *This person is a lot like me.* And if your clients and customers remember your stories, they'll remember you.

LISTEN AND LEAD

Harry S. Truman, thirty-third President of the United States, once said, "Not all readers are leaders, but all leaders are readers." Read. Read a lot and vary your reading material. Keep a good book and magazine by your bedside at all times, and read a few pages each night before you fall asleep. The more you know, the more interesting you will be to others, and everyone loves being around a stimulating conversationalist.

STAY OPEN TO POSSIBILITY

Take a moment and reflect on all the business and social opportunities that have come your way so far in your life, from a new job, promotion, or business venture to friendship, or maybe even love. You just never know when your next great opportunity might present itself, so treat everyone you meet as a potential customer, client, or new best friend. I'm so grateful to have learned this potentially life-changing lesson some years ago.

On a crisp morning in November 1993, my manager at The Breakers asked me to accompany fifteen other employees on an "educational" field trip to the Palm Beach County Solid Waste Authority.

"What's the Solid Waste Authority?" I asked. I already knew that I didn't like the sound of this place.

"It's the county dump," my manager replied with a wry grin on her face.

"Do I have to go?" I moaned.

"Yes, you do," she said. "The hotel is starting a new recycling initiative and I want you to take pictures of our employees while they learn what happens to glass, cans, and paper after it leaves the hotel. I'd also like for you to feature these photographs in our employee newsletter."

Because I worked in public relations, I often photographed our employees and wrote articles for our newsletter, but today was different. Going to the dump and learning about garbage was not on my priority list. I already had a full schedule that day and I knew it would be a complete waste of my time (no pun intended). But despite my reservations, I agreed to board the tour bus with the other hotel staff members, and off we went on our big field trip.

When our bus pulled up at the entrance of the Solid Waste Authority, the double doors opened and a handsome young man with dark hair and broad shoulders stepped aboard. He greeted our group with a warm, "Hello," and flashed his dazzling smile, and suddenly I was smitten. I instantly developed an overpowering interest in trash and the marvels of recycling. This man's name was Brian Gleason.

Immediately following the tour, I wrote Brian a handwritten note and sent it to him. My intent was to keep in touch, but I also wanted to thank him for the tour and tell him how much I enjoyed meeting him. Little did I know that my courteous little note would lead to a first date, and then another, and another. In short, my reluctant trip to learn about recycling led me to an outcome I never could have predicted. Brian and I are now happily married, and it's all because I opened myself up to an experience that I initially wanted to reject.

Who knows what adventures might await you in the near or far-flung future? If you want to cultivate new relationships, scale the corporate ladder, or simply lead a richer, fuller life, be willing to reach out and do things you wouldn't ordinarily do or go places others might typically avoid. You just never know.

Give Relationships Time to Grow

When it comes to building relationships, time and patience are the magic ingredients. When I think about the many ways in which rewarding relationships are worth the wait, I can't help but think of the Chinese bamboo. This remarkable plant is different from all others in its growth pattern. While most plants grow steadily taller over a period of years, the Chinese bamboo takes four years just to break through the ground. For so long nothing appears to be happening at the surface, but something remarkable is taking place underground. The plant is slowly forming a strong root system long before any part of the plant is visible to the human eye.

Then, in the fifth year, an amazing thing happens. The plant sprouts and begins to grow at an astonishing rate. In just five weeks, a bamboo plant can grow as high as ninety feet. And if you were willing to sit still long enough, you could probably watch the plant grow before your eyes.

I like to think that connecting with others follows a similar pattern, though perhaps in a less spectacular way. Whenever you connect with a potential friend, client, or customer, you plant a seed of opportunity, but this seed needs to be cultivated and nurtured before it can grow. Sometimes it takes weeks, months, and perhaps even years in some cases, but if relationships are handled with care and consideration, just like flowers, they bloom. Those who plant and care for the Chinese bamboo know that if they keep watering and fertilizing the ground in a disciplined manner, their plant will eventually break through and flourish. It's the same way with relationships.

Networking works best in a culture of disciplined friendship. It can't be forced, exploited, or imposed. What I think of as "connecting" relies as much (or more) on kindness and karma as on business savvy, job leads, status, or social media skills. When you are genuine and sincere, not only will you want to help others, but you also will attract people who naturally want to help you in return.

Keep your efforts simple. Become interested in others, find out what matters to them, and then center your conversations and follow-up activities around their priorities. A mutually beneficial relationship is one based on trust, respect, and goodwill; the result is a long-term quality connection in which information, assistance, and resources are freely and openly shared. What more could you ask for?

CHAPTER 8

Cultivate Your VIP Relationships

NO MATTER WHAT ACCOMPLISHMENTS YOU MAKE, SOMEBODY HELPED YOU.

— ALTHEA GIBSON, PROFESSIONAL TENNIS PLAYER

When it comes to making and keeping the right connections, it's important to include a few VIPs (Very Important People) in your networking plan. These are the individuals who have the potential of being powerful allies who could help you accomplish your personal and professional goals.

VIPs are busy, successful people. Their time is precious and because of their prominence they can probably do more for you than you can do for them. These are not relationships you want to rush by asking for assistance or favors prematurely. It takes extensive preparation and patience to cultivate relationships with VIPs.

As you probably know, the best way to meet a VIP is through a referral or a personal introduction. A referral ensures that someone who knows and trusts you has already vetted you. This way, the VIP of your choice will be more receptive to meeting and doing business with you. To avoid embarrassing or awkward incidents, you might appreciate knowing that the most success-ful people are so inundated with requests that they won't even consider connecting with someone unless he or she comes through the proper channels.

When I needed endorsements for my first book, *Business Class,* I had no idea how to ask a famous person for a cover blurb. One person I admired was the late Jack Valenti, former president of the Motion Picture Association of America. In 2005, Mr. Valenti made a visit to West Palm Beach to speak at a charity luncheon at Bear Lakes Country Club. I had read in the newspaper that he would be coming to town, and since I hoped he would endorse my book, I picked up the phone and made a reservation to attend the event. Although the ticket price was expensive for me at the time, it was well worth the risk. My hope was to meet Mr. Valenti at the luncheon and give him a copy of my manuscript.

The big day came and, in keeping with my standard practice for any important event or interview, I arrived early. This gives me time to scope out the premises and it ensures that I'm present and prepared for whatever might happen. Upon entering the country club and picking up my name tag, I approached the co-ordinator of the event.

"Would you be so kind and introduce me to Jack Valenti?" I asked. "I have something that I'd like to give him."

In effect, the program coordinator became my "connector" for this event.

"Of course," she replied. "You'll need to approach us as soon as you see the two of us enter the room. If you wait too long, he'll be surrounded by so many people that you might not get the chance to meet him."

I stood close to the door so I wouldn't miss my one and only opportunity. Just before the luncheon started, the coordinator walked in with Mr. Valenti. I quickly walked over to them, just as she had instructed, she made the introduction, and I was able to present my manuscript to him. Jack Valenti was one of the most poised and charming men I've ever met. Although he didn't know me, he acted as if we'd been acquainted for years. He was gracious and elegant and suggested that I follow up with him in a few weeks.

One month later, I followed up with an e-mail. Within minutes after I hit the "send" button, I was elated to receive the first official endorsement for my book, just as I had hoped.

My introduction to this famous man didn't happen by accident. Instead, it took place because I had a plan and I asked for a favor from someone I knew could help me.

Here are several effective ways to facilitate VIP relationships:

- Read everything the person you want to meet has written.

- Read everything that has been written about him or her.

- Read everything that this individual has recommended.

- Check his or her blog or Web site regularly.

- Sign up for his or her newsletter.

- Follow him or her on Twitter.

- Connect with him or her on LinkedIn and Facebook (only after you've established a good relationship).

- Stay in touch regularly by phone or e-mail once you've met the person.

• If you meet with the VIP over a meal, always pick up the tab.

• It's best to wait until you've built a truly solid connection before asking for any favors.

Gracious Gains: How to Properly Ask a VIP for a Favor

In general, VIPs are inundated with requests for referrals and favors and they tend to decline unless they know you well. Once you've established a relationship, you're ready to take the plunge. Your polite requests will be more valid and effective if you are willing to follow these guidelines:

• **Greet the VIP:** If you write a letter or send an e-mail to a VIP, be sure to include his or her name and spell it correctly. Correspondence that lacks the recipient's name is a dead giveaway that you have sent your request to a list of people. Using the person's name shows that you have taken the time to personalize your message.

• **Enlighten the VIP:** VIPs are busy people. Don't assume they will remember you. It's a courtesy to discreetly remind the person about how you met, or how you know each other, or if you share a mutual friend. Did you meet at a luncheon, conference, or seminar? Were you referred by someone? If so, include that in your note. VIPs meet a lot of people every day, so take the initiative and briefly recap the circumstances of your meeting.

• **Flatter the VIP:** VIPs are more apt to help you if you have done something for them. Have you read their books, purchased one of their products, or made contributions to their favorite charities? Have you provided them with a good resource or referred them to someone of importance? When you do something nice for people, they are more willing to reciprocate.

· **Be Specific:** Make sure your favor or request is clear, concise, and contains all the facts or pertinent information; otherwise you may get either a delayed response or none at all.

· **Give the VIP a Deadline:** If you need an answer right away, let the VIP know that your request is time sensitive. Otherwise, you may miss out on an opportunity.

· **Thank the VIP:** If you do receive a personal response (positive or negative), send a thank-you note to express your appreciation for the VIP's efforts. It's always nice to let people know that their efforts were worthwhile and helpful, so explain how the situation turned out if you acted on the advice you were given.

As you begin to cultivate the care and feeding of a VIP relationship, here are some suggestions to keep in mind:

· **Study Up:** Research the VIP's passions. Your correspondence or conversation will flow more smoothly if you know something about his or her hobbies or interests. If you can find something in common with the VIP, the connection will most likely shift your relationship from casual to personal.

· **Show Up:** Making connections just doesn't happen by sitting at home or at your desk waiting for the phone to ring. You need to connect with VIPs early (and often) in your career. It's best not to wait to reach out until you get laid off or need a favor or referral. You'll increase your chances of making a good connection if you're in the right place at the right time with the right information and the right attitude.

• **Pay Up:** In some cases, you may have to stretch your budget and spend some money to gain access to a VIP. Don't be surprised if you have to buy a pricey ticket to a luncheon or gala so you can meet the VIP in person. You'll acquire extra points if you can find out a VIP's favorite cause, charity, or alma mater and make a donation in his or her name. Who knows, you might receive a personal, handwritten thank-you note from the VIP.

• **Speak Up:** Don't be afraid to ask a VIP for a favor or a request, but make sure you know when and how to ask. Approach the VIP in a polite, humble, and respectful manner, and give it a shot. My motto is: if you don't ask, the answer will always be "no," but if you do ask, the answer just might be "yes."

• **Set Up:** It's counterproductive to attend events just because you skipped lunch and you're hungry for cheese puffs or thirsty for a cocktail. Stay focused on your goal. Make a mental list of the VIPs you'd like to meet, and then introduce yourself as soon as you spot them. If possible, connect with the people you want to meet before the meal. Some VIPs like to make an early showing at an event and then quietly slip away as soon as possible so they can get to another engagement. Don't let nerves, procrastination, or hesitation (or hors d'oeuvres) result in a missed opportunity.

• **Buddy Up:** When you want to meet a VIP for the first time, find a host or someone in authority (the "connector") to introduce you. This makes the introduction more significant than if you were to approach the VIP on your own. If there's no connector, then take the initiative and hope for the best. Once you've introduced yourself, ask intelligent questions that will encourage a brief conversation with the VIP. Solicit the VIP's ideas or find out what his or her experience has been. You'll always connect more quickly and deeply when you focus on the other person's interests instead of your own. That's what I call social graces, and they will take you a long way in developing relationships that can make a difference in your professional life.

· **Step Up:** I'd be remiss if I didn't encourage you to put your boss on your VIP list. In a perfect world you might consider treating all of your work colleagues like VIPs, but it makes perfect sense to work especially well with your boss. After all, the person you report to is the one who hands out raises and promotions and has the power over the future of your career. This makes your manager or director a very important person in your life. You will benefit by paying close attention to what your boss does (or doesn't do) and learning all you can about him or her in terms of personality, work style, and values.

Notice how your boss acts on good days and bad, what and whom he or she considers important, and how she or he handles the corporate bureaucracy. Understand your boss's goals and priorities. Identify any areas of weakness or challenges and ask what you can do to help.

Marilyn Murray Willison, author of *The Self-Empowered Woman: 17 Characteristics of High Achievers,* says it's wise to pay particular attention to the things your boss doesn't like to do and then become exceptionally good at those tasks. You'll not only score extra points with your boss; you'll also make yourself indispensable. Your initiative and willingness to go the extra mile might just put you on your boss's VIP list as well.

CHAPTER 9

Hone Your Business Hospitality Skills

THERE IS AN EMANATION FROM THE HEART IN GENUINE HOSPITALITY WHICH CANNOT BE DESCRIBED, BUT IS IMMEDIATELY FELT, AND PUTS THE STRANGER AT ONCE AT HIS EASE.

— WASHINGTON IRVING, AUTHOR, ESSAYIST, AND BIOGRAPHER

Growing up in Florida, I was taught the value of hospitality, particularly "Southern" hospitality. When I think back to my childhood roots, many summertime images come to mind—sweet tea, front porches, Sunday dinners with friends and family, a meticulous table setting, orange blossoms, a train whistle blowing in the distance, and the inevitable bloodthirsty mosquitoes.

Despite our modest means, my mother was a brilliant host. This was because her primary concern always centered on her guests. She always wanted the guests in her home to feel welcome, happy, and, most of all, well fed. Fortunately, like most Southern women, she was an excellent cook. Mom made the most delectable and mouthwatering roast beef, conch peas, and mashed potatoes, as well as fried pork chops with rice and tomato gravy.

Over the years, I'm certain that I inherited my love for cooking and entertaining from watching the women in my family lovingly prepare their simple yet delicious meals. They taught me the truth about entertaining. Hospitality has nothing to do with spending large amounts of money on food and decorations or coming up with clever ways of impressing people. To be a good host, all you need is some basic skills, adequate time to prepare, an open mind, and, most of all, a welcoming spirit.

In some way, we all entertain for business at different times in our lives. It may be as simple as inviting a coworker into your home for a cup of coffee and a snack, inviting a visiting colleague to share a sandwich and soda in your office, dining with your boss at a nearby café, or treating a client to a cool beverage at the nineteenth hole after a round of golf.

Regardless of the venue, all entertaining involves some form of hospitality, and hospitality is all about grace and style interwoven with a deep appreciation for stimulating conversation and congenial company. Entertaining is a blend of many honorable virtues that have passed through the generations—gentility, kindness, and a welcoming appreciation for others based on an open, caring heart and mind-set.

Simply put, entertaining is the gentle art of sharing. It is the noble gesture of putting another's comfort before your own by taking the time to make others feel good about themselves. Whether you're on the giving or receiving end, a hefty helping of hospitality inevitably makes you feel good and can make your clients, colleagues, and coworkers feel important and cared for.

All of us will entertain at some point, and it will usually begin at a casual, almost organic level with friends. But entertaining for business becomes important (even obligatory) if you regularly accept invitations from others. If you allow yourself to be entertained without responding in kind, you could be perceived as someone who takes but doesn't give. No matter what your occupation or goals may be, there exist many reasons and opportunities to entertain. Here are just a few:

- To repay others for their hospitality

- To cement friendships or form new ones

- To share both your culinary and hosting talents

- To showcase the charms of your home or hometown

- To celebrate a special occasion or to honor a particular person

- To get better acquainted with coworkers, colleagues, and potential mentors

Conversely, some people host parties as an attempt to curry favor, to look good, or to climb up a few notches on the corporate ladder. Perhaps you've attended a few of these events. But the key to being a hospitable host is all about making your guests the focus rather than yourself. In other words, if you entertain for all the right reasons, your genuine, warmhearted hospitality will be apparent to all.

Effortless Entertaining

Want to create deeper levels of intimacy and stronger connections with coworkers, customers, and clients? Find ways to entertain in a casual, low-maintenance atmosphere. You'll be surprised how you can discover unknown aspects of someone's personality by engaging in a relaxing dinner or by meeting for a drink or two after work rather than having any number of in-office meetings. We naturally loosen up outside the office and automatically slip into being more of ourselves. A change of scenery, a casual venue, and maybe a bit of wine (in moderation) set the stage for relating at a completely different level. It's astonishing how much more you can learn about someone when you are both doing something you enjoy.

EFFICIENT ENTERTAINING ON THE ROAD

My love for food, enjoyment of people, and frequent trips for business meetings have helped me enhance my organizational skills. There was a time when I'd wear myself out trying to meet with a long list of potential clients or colleagues I wanted to see. I finally learned that instead of scheduling a series of individual lunches with several people over the course of a few days, I could consolidate my social schedule and save myself a lot of hassle and hustle.

A few years ago, when I attended an image consultants' conference in Tampa, Florida, I needed to see five people in three days, but I had seminars to attend. With a limited amount of time for socializing I knew it would be impossible to see everyone. Then I realized I could invite everyone to join me for a dinner and that way I wouldn't have to sacrifice a seminar or a meeting with someone I truly wanted to see.

I always figure that a nice mix of different professions and personalities can be the perfect recipe for a terrific gathering. Each "guest" can benefit from meeting the others, and I'll be able to catch up with all of them and perhaps even garner some future business opportunities.

In his book *Never Eat Alone*, Keith Ferrazzi says that he manages his time and appointments by constantly looking to include others in whatever he is doing. "Sometimes I'll take potential employees for a workout and conduct the interview over a run," he writes. "I'll occasionally ask a few employees to share a car ride with me to the airport." Ferrazzi has figured out that this form of multitasking is inexpensive and it keeps him connected with different parts of his "community."

Like me, you may have already discovered that the Internet is an outstanding and economical resource to stay connected and build relationships. While I was on a recent trip to Charleston, South Carolina, I posted an announcement on Twitter that I would be coming to town for business and would love to meet some of my Charleston-based Twitter contacts. Before long, one of my followers named Laura Otero (whom I had never met) tweeted that she loved the idea of getting together and would like to invite a few more people for a "tweet-up." Laura contacted eight of her Twitter friends and invited them to a "Meet the Etiquette Expert Jacqueline Whitmore" cocktail party at the lovely rooftop Pavilion Bar overlooking the harbor and the cityscape. It turned out to be a fun-filled evening, everyone was responsible for paying for their own meal, and I made some wonderful new friends and business connections.

Tweet-ups can be held virtually anywhere—a private dining room at a local restaurant, a scenic park, and even a bowling alley. Whether you're new to the workforce or a seasoned professional, look for any and every opportunity to build relationships and expand your sphere of influence. All it takes is a little planning and ingenuity.

A Toast from the Host

When it comes to hosting an event, it doesn't have to be elaborate or expensive. If you're on a budget or if you're new to the world of entertaining, you might try organizing a group lunch at a local diner or pizza parlor. Invite a few friends to meet you after work for happy hour at a sports bar or a popular watering hole or organize a picnic lunch complete with sandwiches, chips, and sodas if you live near the mountains or the beach. When you feel more adventuresome and if you have the space to accommodate guests, host a casual dinner for two or three of your colleagues in your home.

It took me a couple of years after I got married before I was courageous enough to host an event for more than three or four people. After many years of practice, I'm now much more comfortable with the notion of hosting larger, more important events. For example, twice a year, I hold marketing retreats at my home in Palm Beach for up to ten etiquette and image consultants. The participants attend meetings at my house during the day and stay overnight at a nearby bed-and-breakfast.

On the first day of the retreat, I invite my attendees to join me in the late afternoon on a sunset beach walk. This change of scene gives us all a chance to kick back and switch gears. I bring a cooler containing wine, bottles of water and soda, and a few plastic glasses so my guests have a choice of beverages. I've found that when you combine the relaxing sound of the ocean, the soft white sand beneath your bare feet, and a refreshing glass of crisp sauvignon blanc or sparkling soda, the stress of the day or week quickly fades away.

On our retreat beach walks, we don't talk business at all.

Instead, we share stories about our families and our lives, we toast one another, and we laugh and relax. It makes for an excellent bonding experience.

I encourage you to look for opportunities to include others in the things you love to do. Whether it's a scenic hike, a sporting event or concert, a grand opening, a book signing, afternoon tea at an elegant hotel, or any other activity, there's a deep-seated joy in getting to share your passion with others and witnessing their appreciation of it.

FASHION YOUR PASSION

What are you most passionate about? Consider how you can build an event around one of your passions as a unique and refreshing means of engaging new contacts or maintaining existing ones. If you love the theater, invite potential and current clients and customers to a show. From nature walks to ice-cream socials, or blues concerts to ballets, what you do isn't as important as how you feel about it. Do something you enjoy and it will be obvious to your guests.

When your day or week is fueled by passion and filled with interesting people to share it with, branching out into new venues and experiences will simply be a natural extension of the way you connect with new people or continue enhancing your established relationships.

CHAPTER 10

Entertain with Elegance and Ease

**THAT'S THE SECRET OF ENTERTAINING. YOU MAKE
YOUR GUESTS FEEL WELCOME AND AT HOME.
IF YOU DO THAT HONESTLY, THE REST
TAKES CARE OF ITSELF.**

— BARBARA HALL, WRITER AND TELEVISION PRODUCER

Entertaining clients, customers, and coworkers in a restaurant can be a lot of fun, but did you know that one of the most generous gifts you can give to others is an invitation to your home? When you entertain in your home, you reveal a more personal side of yourself, which in turn can build camaraderie and trust with your guests. My husband, Brian, and I love our home and we take a great deal of pride in sharing it with others. Our house is neither big nor fancy, but it is comfortable, tastefully decorated, and we always have something good to eat on hand.

It's not necessary to be a gourmet chef or a professional party planner to coordinate a casual or elegant event. All you need is a little bit of planning and preparation and an adventurous spirit. I've learned that the best host is someone who entertains with heart and soul and happily pays attention to the details. The first step is to be as organized as possible to keep your plans from going awry. Unfortunately, many of us learn this important lesson from experience, and my hope is to help make you look good and avoid embarrassment regardless of how much or how little you entertain.

Before you invite your boss or an important client over for dinner, it's best to practice on your friends first. Friends tend to be less discerning and more forgiving. During the early years of our marriage, Brian and I needed some practice, so we decided to host a dinner party for a few of our friends. My first mistake was deciding to serve something I had never cooked before—beef tenderloin. My second mistake was asking Brian how long he thought it would take to partially sear it on the grill and then finish baking it in the oven. He said it would take approximately forty-five minutes total.

Today I know better than to ask my husband for cooking advice, and here's why. Our guests arrived and the tenderloin was still rare. (It needed at least another hour to cook.) I hadn't planned on serving any hors d'oeuvres, but I found myself frantically scrounging around in my pantry until I found a half-eaten bag of chips and some stale nuts. Out of necessity, I served these humble munchies to my guests while plying them with a few extra cocktails until the meal was finally ready to serve. Fortunately, our friends still had a good time and never knew that a culinary catastrophe was narrowly avoided.

If something like this happens to you, keep your anxiety to yourself and your guests will never notice. Let go of the need to be perfect, embrace your sense of humor, laugh at yourself, and, I promise, you *will* get through it. Entertaining a few friends can be a good dress rehearsal before you have to put on a big show for important clients or colleagues. You'll know how to set the stage and serve something you've had success with in the past, and like me, you'll know where not to go for cooking advice.

TOP TEN TIPS TO BEING THE HOSPITABLE HOST

Rest assured, in today's fast-paced world, where most of us are short on time and resources, there are no absolute rules about parties. But the best rule to keep in mind is the five Ps: *prior planning prevents poor performance.* After all, the purpose of entertaining for business or pleasure is to show your guests a good time without getting too stressed out. Here are ten tips to help you get started.

1. **Do your homework.** Find out ahead of time if any of your guests have food allergies or other dietary restrictions and plan your menu accordingly or prepare a buffet with a variety of items from which to choose. My advice is to keep it simple and serve what you know. Don't be like me and try to serve an unfamiliar, complicated, or labor-intensive dish your first time out, especially if you are entertaining your boss or an important client. One of your tried-and-true recipes is best. If you want to live on the wild side and serve something exotic or extra special, prepare it at least two or three times before you decide to serve it to guests.

2. **Keep a list.** Just as you would with a business plan, write down all of the items you need to make your meal complete. It's especially frustrating when you think you have all of your ingredients and then discover in the midst of cooking that you don't

have enough salt, sugar, or butter. If that happens, I hope you have a good relationship with your neighbors, or you'll be making a mad dash to the store at the last minute.

3. Have a variety of beverages on hand. The mark of a good host is to have a few bottles of red and white wine along with plenty of nonalcoholic beverages for the teetotalers in the group.

4. Stock up on snacks. This includes nuts, chips, salsa or dip, one or two different cheeses, crackers, and one or two kinds of frozen appetizers. Choose hors d'oeuvres that are easy to eat and require only one bite. This will ensure that no one gets crumbs on his or her nice outfit or on your floor.

5. Do as much as possible the day before. I like to set my table the night before. I also prefer to clean and polish my serving pieces and fill my salt and pepper shakers a few days before the party to avoid last-minute flurries.

6. Iron your linens. When you are serving cocktails, provide linen cocktail napkins or, at the very least, decorative paper cocktail napkins. For dinners, I prefer linen napkins because they're more elegant than paper ones.

7. Set the mood. Candles are an easy, inexpensive, quick way to make any home more inviting. And we all know that everyone *and* everything looks better by candlelight. Buy as many candles as you can and place them throughout your house. Remember to reserve a few unscented ones for the dinner table. Light your candles approximately fifteen or twenty minutes prior to your guests'

arrival, and then light the candles on your dinner table just before everyone sits down to dine.

8. Choose your tunes. Music is a vital element in the staging
of a good dinner party, as it sets the tone for the evening. Create a
dinner party playlist on your iPod or iPhone or preset your CD
player so there's music in the air when your guests arrive and keep
it playing throughout the evening.

9. Preset your coffee and tea service. About an hour before
your party, set up your coffeemaker and put cream, milk, sugar,
and sweetener in decorative containers. Put condiments in attractive bowls or containers rather than placing bottles directly
on the table. Put your coffee cups, saucers, teaspoons, and assorted
teas on a tray on a side table.

10. Keep fragrant items off the table. Scented candles and
flowers can compete with and even overpower food aromas. I say
this on behalf of anyone who's ever been overwhelmed by the
scent of stargazer lilies or a scented pine candle while attempting
to enjoy dinner.

Bonus tip: Make time for yourself. Allow plenty of time to
shower, get dressed, and look your best for your party. You'll want
to greet your guests at the door with a relaxed smile on your face.
The more prepared you are, the more comfortable you will feel,
and the better time you'll have at your own party.

Sensible Seating Arrangements

A nice mix of different professions and personalities can be the perfect recipe for a terrific dinner party. Whether you're entertaining at home or in a restaurant, it's important to put some thought into the seating arrangements. Avoid the overly casual "just sit anywhere," because this can put people in an awkward position. Pay special attention to the chemistry between your guests. If you know your guests well, you'll have a sense of who will blend well with whom, and that's why place cards are a great option. The nice thing about place cards is that everyone knows where they should sit the minute they approach the table; otherwise, you may have to quickly direct your guests to their proper seats. Another advantage of place cards is that when guests see their names they can't help but feel special and welcome.

The order in which your guests are served depends on whether it's a social or business event. If you are hosting a business dinner, seat your guests according to rank and status. You should sit at the head of the table and your guest of honor (if there is one) should sit on your right side. Serve your guest of honor first and then proceed to serve your other guests in a counterclockwise direction. In social situations, women are served first. Protocol dictates that the host and hostess are always served last.

Here are some seating tips to help make the table talk flow smoothly:

- Separate couples. Protocol and common sense decree that guests who are married or living together should not sit next to each other. I once made the mistake of putting a married couple together at a dinner party and they bickered all evening. The exception to the "couple rule" is if two people are engaged they may sit next to each other.

· Seat the most talkative person in the middle, preferably next to a shy person.

· When two tables are used, sit at one table and seat your cohost (if you have one) at another table. When there are three or more tables, assign a table host to each table.

Wine Wisdom 101

Did you know that the old adage about serving white wine with fish or chicken and red wine with red meat no longer applies? If you're in a restaurant, it's always better to order what you like and what you think your guests will enjoy than to follow this outdated rule. In my home, I offer both red and white wine and then I let my guests choose whatever they prefer.

If your guests don't drink alcohol, offer a nonalcoholic beverage and refrain from making any comment about their choice. People can become very uncomfortable if someone makes an issue about their not imbibing.

If you know that your guests enjoy a glass of wine or two with dinner and you want to appear more knowledgeable about wine, you'll appreciate the following tips. To help me compile the most accurate information, I conferred with Mark Spivak, wine expert and author of *The Affordable Wine Guide to California and the Pacific Northwest*.

· It's a host's responsibility to choose the wine in a restaurant. It's wise not to let your guests choose because they might order something out of your price range or outside the limits of your expense account. If you decide to show off and order the most expensive bottle of wine, you may be sending the wrong message to your guests. You don't want them to think that you're the type to spend money carelessly or take advantage of an expense account. If you're not sure what to order, choose something moderately priced or ask the sommelier for a recommendation. If you want to stay within a certain price range, discreetly point to a price on the wine menu and ask the sommelier, "Do you mind recommending something in this region?" (Your guests won't know what you're pointing to.)

· There's no need to fill your guest's glass all the way to the top. Allow enough room to swirl the wine and appreciate all the nuances of the bouquet. Remember to hold both red and white wine glasses by the stem (rather than the bowl) to avoid transferring odors such as perfume to the glass.

· Wine won't really "breathe" after you open the bottle, given the small amount of air that can interact with the wine once the cork is pulled. That's why it's best to pour red wine into a decanter before it's consumed. There are three traditional reasons to decant: to separate older wine from its sediment, to aerate younger wine, and to raise the temperature of a bottle taken from a cold cellar. If you're serving a young Cabernet, Syrah, or blend, decant it about an hour ahead of time. Many sommeliers automatically decant all younger reds. Older wines are much trickier. The older the bottle, the less time you should allow for aeration, as the wine will deteriorate when exposed to air. Be especially careful with anything older than ten years, particularly if it's a more delicate variety, such as a Pinot Noir.

• It doesn't happen often, but it's possible that you might occasionally get a bad bottle of wine. The mark of a contaminated bottle is unmistakable. Sniff the wine (never the cork) after it is poured, and if you notice a foul or "off" aroma that resembles a wet, moldy basement or sweaty gym socks return it or send it back if you're in a restaurant.

Your Serve

The secret to elegant entertaining is surprisingly simple: Be artfully attentive. If you are hosting a large party, don't be afraid to delegate. If you have an experienced friend or colleague who offers to help, say yes. If not, consider hiring someone to help you set up, serve drinks, take coats, and clean up, so you can shower your guests with attention.

With a little planning, preparation, and organization, you can create a relaxed, hospitable atmosphere where everything will fall into place. Don't waste precious time running back and forth to the kitchen throughout the evening. The dirty dishes can wait until after everyone departs.

Your guests are there to enjoy being with you, and chances are, they'll enjoy many of the other people they'll meet. And thanks to your welcoming tone and attention to detail, your guests will be eternally grateful you invited them, and so will you.

CHAPTER 11

Be the World's Best Guest

**IT IS NOT THE QUANTITY OF THE MEAT, BUT
THE CHEERFULNESS OF THE GUESTS,
WHICH MAKES THE FEAST.**
— EDWARD HYDE, ENGLISH HISTORIAN AND STATESMAN

Nothing is more nerve-wracking or humiliating than speaking in front of a bunch of boisterous and intoxicated individuals. Several years ago I was hired by a corporation to teach a dining-etiquette course at one of the nicest waterfront restaurants in Fort Lauderdale. The CEO told me that his staff would gather at 5:30 p.m., board his private yacht, and then set sail for the restaurant. I drove to the restaurant, arrived at 7:00 p.m. as instructed, and shortly thereafter the yacht pulled up to the dock and the group disembarked. Many of them seemed to swagger and teeter up the stairs where our event would take place. Everyone was in an especially jovial mood, and it took me a few minutes to figure out why. For the last hour and a half the group had enjoyed unlimited cocktails and hors d'oeuvres while en route to the restaurant. By the time they arrived, they had more than a good buzz going and couldn't wait to order dinner and more drinks. As the night went on, they continued to get more intoxicated and less interested in my dining-etiquette seminar. Understandably, I cut my presentation short.

The line between professional and social events is often quite blurred when it comes to the workplace, and even more so when both are combined. Attending a social gathering with clients, customers, and coworkers can be a great opportunity to make a positive impression on the people who have their eye on you at work, or it can be a career killer for the unfortunate ones who let loose, lose focus, and act as if they're at a local bar. While some companies may have explicit rules about professional decorum when it comes to work-related social events, most of us are left to our own devices.

Pass the Guest Test

To ensure that you stay in the good graces of others (and that you don't sabotage your professional opportunities), here are a few simple, yet often forgotten, tips to follow. Remember these courtesies when you are invited to an office party, someone's home, a fund raiser, a restaurant, a special event, or anywhere else.

• **Respond promptly.** If you receive an invitation, it's a courtesy to respond as soon as possible. If you wait longer than one week, it might look like you're holding out for a more attractive option. Far too many hosts have shared with me how frustrating it is (not to mention a waste of time) having to call their guests in order to find out if they'll be attending.

• **Show up.** If you accept an invitation to an event, keep your word unless there's a personal emergency. In that case, immediately inform your host that you won't be able to attend. There may be times when unavoidable circumstances prevent you from staying for the entire event, and in that case tell your host beforehand that regrettably you must leave. If you give anything other than a truthful, reasonable excuse, you may not get invited back.

• **Ask permission before bringing an uninvited guest.** When in doubt, simply ask the host or the organizer, "Are guests included?" If you're permitted to bring someone, choose your companion carefully. An ill-mannered, inappropriately dressed guest or misfit can reflect poorly on you.

• **Bring a small gift.** If you're invited to someone's home, show your appreciation. Some popular gifts include assorted teas or coffees, hot cocoa mix, a bottle of wine or champagne, a fragrant candle, a box of truffles, imported olive oil, unique jams or chutneys, or some handmade goodies. Insert a small card with your name on it inside the gift so the host will know who brought it. It's best not to bring flowers wrapped in cellophane because it means work for the host, who will have to leave his or her guests and find a vase. It's more convenient to send flowers either the day of or the day after the party. If you bring a bottle of wine, don't assume that the host will serve it. He or she has probably already selected a wine to complement the meal and will likely decide to save yours for another occasion.

• **Be mindful of your portions.** Piling hors d'oeuvres on your cocktail napkin or plate as each server goes by is a faux pas. When hors d'oeuvres or appetizers are offered, it's helpful to remember to concentrate more on mingling than on the meatballs. Select foods that are easy to eat and won't get stuck in your teeth or give you bad breath. Always keep breath mints in your pocket or handbag, and pop one in your mouth before you introduce yourself and shake hands with someone. If you're holding a cold, wet glass, it's essential to keep it in your left hand to avoid giving someone a cold, clammy handshake.

• **Circulate.** Go out of your way to introduce yourself to a variety of people. Diversification is the hallmark of an investment portfolio, and the same holds true in networking and relationship management. If you attend an office event, be sure to meet people at different levels of your organization, especially those from different departments with whom you might interact from a distance but whom you have never met. If it's an off-site event, be open and friendly to everyone; the person you connect with today could end up being your best client or customer or boss in the future.

• **Take your assigned seat.** Never, ever move place cards at the table to suit your mood or desires. If you want to sit next to someone or at a special table, call your host ahead of time and make your request.

• **Eat what you can and leave the rest.** If you're served something you don't like, push it around a bit on your plate and focus on the conversation. Or take a small bite; you might be pleasantly surprised. Avoid making a big issue of your likes, dislikes, food sensitivities, or preferences and refrain from making personal remarks that may put your host (or yourself) in a bad light. Just enjoy what you can eat and appreciate the social aspects surrounding you. If you don't eat certain foods for ethical, medical, or religious reasons, it's important to let your host know ahead of time. You might graciously say something like, "Ned, I'm following a vegetarian diet. I'm sure there will be plenty for me to eat; however, I'm happy to bring a dish to share."

· **Keep the conversation upbeat.** Let's face it, few of us are big on making small talk with strangers, but there are some things you can do to make it easier. Stand close to the door and greet other guests as they walk in, approach a person who is sitting or standing alone, or introduce yourself to a group of three or more. Never interrupt two people who seem to be engrossed in conversation. When you are at a loss for words, you might start out by saying something like, "How do you know the host or hostess?" "What do you think about the decorations?" or, "Did you try the delicious pot stickers?" That should get you rolling.

Restaurants, movies, books, local events, and hobbies are all acceptable topics for social gatherings, as are current events. Subjects best avoided include money, religion, sex, and politics. Not only is it bad manners to badmouth coworkers, clients, or, worse, the boss; it also could be disastrous. If someone brings up a hot-button issue that sparks controversy or disagreement, quietly take your leave and seek shelter while the negative people rain on their own parade. If some wise guy (and there's always one in the crowd) brings up a potentially incendiary topic or launches into an off-putting joke, ignore it as best you can and excuse yourself. If you are speaking to a conversational rambler and you feel trapped, try to change the subject, keep the exchange brief, and then move on whenever you get the chance.

· **Keep your food to yourself.** When you're dining with friends in a restaurant, it may seem like the polite thing to do to exchange small samplings of the different dishes brought to the table, but it can be messy and sometimes awkward, especially if someone at the table would rather not share. If your colleagues insist on sampling one another's food, ask the server for two or three small, clean plates and transfer samples onto those plates using clean utensils.

It's best not to exchange food after everyone has begun eating, as this becomes an issue of hygiene rather than good manners.

• **Eat, drink, and be merry (but not too merry).** There always seem to be a few people in any given social gathering who feel compelled to show everyone else just how much they can drink and how loudly they can talk. I witnessed this firsthand when I worked at The Breakers. My coworkers and I frequently attended lavish parties complete with open bars. One night our sales and marketing department held a celebration dinner that included cocktails as well as several bottles of wine. After dinner, we went downstairs to play some pool and some of the members in our group decided to light up cigars and take part in a scotch and brandy party. As a result of all the drinking, several of the more senior, uninhibited associates became amorous and started flirting with the women in the group, particularly the twentysomethings.

Needless to say, the same perpetrators were dragging at work the next day, and those who suffered from hangovers had to endure embarrassing blow-by-blow descriptions of their transgressions. Obviously, it makes sense to have a glass of wine or a cocktail at events, but drink in moderation. I've seen too many promising executives prematurely sink their careers (and friendships) due to their lack of restraint. The best rule of thumb is to maintain a sober state of mind. Don't risk ruining your reputation, because your behavior is always being evaluated by someone. Too much liquid cheer can lead to regretful (and sometimes fatal) situations.

• **Don't be afraid to just say "no thank you."** If you don't drink alcohol, you have the right to confidently and cordially decline when it's offered. It's not necessary to launch into any kind of excuse or explanation or to tell your host that you're taking medication, are on a diet, or are in recovery. Order a club soda with lime or ginger ale in a champagne glass to fit in and avoid the need for explanations.

• **Dress professionally, not provocatively.** The appropriate outfit and attitude are crucial to your career advancement. If you're not sure about the dress code, ask the host or the person who invited you to the event.

• **Thank the host.** When it's time to leave, thank your host in person, and then follow up with a written thank-you note or a phone call the next day.

How to Navigate a Business Meal

For many of us, wining and dining clients and customers is a part of our job, whether it's over a power lunch or a formal dinner. Keep these ten tidbits in mind whether you're hosting or being hosted at a business meal:

1. **Before choosing a restaurant,** find out about your guests' food and location preference. Choose a quiet restaurant so you can carry on a conversation without straining to hear one another.

2. **Pay for the meal** if you are the person who did the inviting. One of the savviest etiquette tricks in the book is to take care of the bill before it arrives at your table. You arrive at the restaurant early, introduce yourself to the manager or the maître d', and then request that the check not be brought to your table. As the business meal comes to a close,

excuse yourself as if you're going to the restroom and pay the bill. If you and your company have a working relationship with a particular restaurant, you may even want to set up a corporate account or call the restaurant ahead of time and give the manager your credit card number over the phone.

3. **Eat a little something before you arrive** at the restaurant. Remember: a business meal is more about the business of building relationships and less about the meal.

4. **Start off with some casual chitchat** instead of moving into business topics right away. Gradually shift into the purpose of your meeting as the meal progresses. Before dessert arrives, ease into casual conversation once again, so you end the meeting on a relaxed and positive note.

5. **Avoid foods that are messy** and complicated to eat, like spaghetti with a red sauce, barbeque ribs, oversized sandwiches, or lobster in the shell.

6. **Don't place your cell phone on the table** and then glance down at it every time it pings or vibrates. Silence your device and keep it out of sight until you leave the restaurant. Keep other personal items such as your handbag, car keys, or eyeglasses off the table as well.

7. **If you leave the table momentarily,** place your napkin on your chair, rather than displaying it on the table for all your guests to see. When you finish your meal, place the napkin neatly to the left of your plate.

8. **Pace yourself so you don't finish eating** before your dining companions. If you are the first to finish, don't allow your server to remove your plate until your companions have finished eating.

9. **Don't order coffee** or dessert unless your companion does, too.

10. **For Men Only:** Keep your jacket on during dinner. The only exception to this rule is if the host removes his jacket first. Help your female dining companions with their chairs. If you're attending a social event, the correct procedure is to help the woman on your right first and then the woman on your left. It's also a nice gesture to stand whenever a woman leaves or returns to the table. I guarantee that these simple courtesies will set you apart from other men in the room who don't know or don't bother with small gestures. For strict business meetings where the environment is gender neutral, it's nice, but not necessary, to assist a woman with her chair in a restaurant. In many fine restaurants, the server will do this.

Being a good guest means putting your best foot forward and keeping it there; everything you say and do can either help or hinder your professional image and the relationships you've painstakingly developed. Have fun and be yourself, but remember that too much "fun" could result in more trouble than you can imagine. A little bit of conscious restraint on your part can make a big difference in maintaining the professional reputation you've worked so hard to establish, and it's the easiest way to keep your career path on solid ground as well.

PART THREE

PROFESSIONALISM

CHAPTER 12

Social Media Essentials

**WHAT YOU DO SPEAKS SO LOUDLY THAT
I CANNOT HEAR WHAT YOU SAY.**

— Ralph Waldo Emerson, American essayist,
lecturer, and poet

We all know that first impressions can be lasting impressions. This conventional wisdom applies to how we present ourselves not only in person but online as well. Now more than ever, millions of people choose to do business by researching a company or an individual online. Whether you know it or not, people immediately judge us on our Web site or blog design and by what we post on our social-networking sites. Let's take a look at some of the most popular tools you can use to market yourself on the Internet.

Your Web Site and Blog

When they are designed correctly, your blog and Web site can be extremely beneficial for building your business. My Web site is my number one marketing tool. If you Google "etiquette expert," my Web site appears at the top of the rankings, and this is how most of my prospective clients find me.

Web sites are great, but many businesses and entrepreneurs are switching to or adding blogs as a means of self-promotion. Some people blog to share their ideas and opinions, while others blog as a way to inform, educate, or entertain. For example, if you visit my blog (http://jacquelinewhitmore.com) you'll see that I post tips, articles, and videos that are related to etiquette. Blogs are also a great way to reflect our expertise and areas of interest.

Whether you plan to have a Web site or blog (or both), make sure that you are getting the maximum results. Within ten seconds or less, others evaluate your blog or Web site on these five key factors:

• **Performance:** Does the page load quickly? If your site takes more than ten seconds to load, people may get frustrated and abandon the page altogether.

• **Credibility:** Are you a reliable source? Most people want to get their information from an expert. Educate and entertain by posting video blogs (or vlogs) and articles of interest.

• **Usability:** Make sure your content is organized and easily accessible. If people can't easily navigate from one item to another, they'll bail on you. Time is precious, and if visitors can't find what they need when they need it, they'll move on to your competitor's site.

• **Relevancy:** Does your site have what your prospects are looking for? Pay attention to which pages receive the most traffic and which posts receive the most comments, and offer more content like that. For example, I notice that I receive more comments whenever I post one of my favorite recipes or give away a product.

While you don't need to offer daily posts, vow to keep your Web site or blog fresh, updated, and informative so your visitors have a reason to keep coming back.

• **Your E-mail Address:** A lot of people don't realize that their e-mail address is a significant part of their online personal brand. If you're job-searching or communicating with customers or clients online, make sure that every aspect of your e-mail connotes a professional image. An e-mail identity like master-blaster@gmail.com doesn't sound as professional as Janice .Jones@gmail.com. If you have a Web site, consider using your name followed by your URL: Ted@TedSmithAutomotive.com.

Become an Invaluable Online Resource

Many years ago, before any of us ever heard the term "social networking," we would attend events, collect business cards, and then (if we remembered or had the time) enter our contacts' names into our computers. If we were at all organized and not too terribly busy, we might keep in touch with those contacts from time to time.

There are hundreds of social-networking sites, but currently the most popular are LinkedIn, Facebook, and Twitter. Regardless of which social network you choose to use, each (or all) can go a long way toward building your own brand. Here are some examples of how social media can work in your favor if used appropriately.

LinkedIn

LinkedIn is one of the largest online networking sites on the Web, and if you're interested in building your professional network and growing your business you can profit immensely from its use. Most serious businesspeople have a LinkedIn profile nowadays. Use it to update others on your career accomplishments, to search for job opportunities, and to connect with friends, clients, customers, and colleagues.

Be selective when choosing your contacts. Unlike other networking sites, you should use LinkedIn to connect only with people you know and trust. That way, you can recommend contacts because you actually know them; this protects your reputation and gives credibility to any recommendations you make or opinions you express.

Facebook

Facebook is an effective tool if you want to stay in touch with family and friends, especially those you haven't seen or heard from since elementary school; plus Facebook friends make the best focus group in the world. If I need help solving an unusual dilemma, I will poll my Facebook friends, and they happily give me their opinions. Facebook is also a great place to exchange ideas, share opinions, and keep in touch.

Everyone loves pictures and Facebook allows you to post photos of yourself and your friends on your wall. But keep in mind that unless you customize your privacy settings to "friends only," anyone (including current or potential employers) can view them. Did you know that many employers check out prospective employees' Facebook pages before and after an interview? Some employers also frequently monitor employees' Facebook walls in case they post negative comments about the company. Your wall is a page in your profile that lets others know what you're doing, thinking, or feeling, so it's a good idea to exercise some restraint and discretion in what you post. If you wouldn't want to see your post featured as a headline on the front page of your local newspaper, don't put it on Facebook.

You've probably seen photos of friends making obscene gestures, dancing on tabletops with scantily clad men or women, chugging beer at tailgate parties, or engaging in other speculative activities. You don't want to compromise yourself or your reputation in that way. If you don't want to delete any photos, adjust your privacy settings so only certain people can see them.

Twitter

One of the things I value most about Twitter is the way it allows me to tap into an amazing community of people from around the world with whom I share similar interests. I've often said, "Facebook is for connecting with people you know; Twitter is for connecting with people you'd like to know."

I use Twitter in a variety of ways. First, I use it for collaboration, networking, and to engage with other interesting and insightful people. Some of these interactions have led to new ideas. For example, when I was recently in New York City I tweeted: "Can anyone recommend a good Indian restaurant in NYC?" As a result, many people responded with excellent suggestions.

Not only does Twitter open up new relationships; it's also a great way to promote our own and other people's content. You can ask questions, share advice or information, and stay abreast of trends in your industry.

Twitter is also a great place to maintain and deepen existing relationships. For example, after an Association of Image Consultants International (AICI) conference in Orlando, I was delighted to find out how many of the members were on Twitter.

When I returned home, I followed up with quite a few members whom I had met in person, and some of us have become regular Twitter buddies.

Finally, I'm always interested in ways to drive traffic to my Web site and blog. If I write an interesting article on my blog, I'll tweet about it and include a link to the article. This, too, helps me extend my reach and widen my readership.

Are You Practicing Proper Social-Networking Etiquette?

Here's a list of etiquette tips for social networking aimed to polish the professional networker.

LinkedIn

· **Showcase your professionalism.** Think of your profile as your individual marketing platform; it needs to reflect your work experiences, achievements, and recognition. Unlike other social-networking sites, LinkedIn is more formal. It's not the place to post casual status updates, rant about past employers, or go into detail about your personal life. Keep your profile public so your colleagues can connect with you. And since pictures are worth a thousand words, post a current and professional photograph of yourself.

· **Connect only with people you know.** Your connections should be able to attest to your quality of work and business practices, and vice versa.

· **Craft a personal note when requesting a connection.** Instead of using the template greeting, remind your prospective contact how you know each other. If you wish to link one of your connections to another, explain how they are connected to you, any commonality they may share, and how they might benefit from knowing each other.

· **Remember that recommendations should reflect a person's work ethic, attitude, and potential for success.** You boost a person's credibility whenever you write a strong recommendation. You have to give recommendations to get them. If you are willing to put in the time and effort to endorse others, you increase the chances of others writing recommendations about you.

· **Keep people up-to-date on your latest work.** Frequently update your profile to keep people informed about your current research, projects, publications, or awards. Doing this will allow your connections to track your progress and support your accomplishments.

Facebook

· **Don't be offended if someone ignores your friend request.** A lot of people try to limit their Facebook network to personal contacts. Others may only use Facebook for specific purposes, like finding local events or staying in touch with long-distance friends and relatives.

· **Customize your privacy settings.** As a Facebook user, you can tailor your privacy settings so everyone or just certain people on your friends list have access to what you post. For example, if you don't want your boss to see pictures of you outside of the work setting or you don't want an old flame to see whom you are dating, you can block that information from him or her.

· **Think twice before you post.** When you post something on Facebook, people can save it or send it to others over the

Internet. You may have read articles or watched TV shows about people losing their jobs over something they posted online; it's just not worth the risk.

· **Remove a friend as a last resort.** People can get offended or hurt when they notice they're missing from your friends list. Try to increase your privacy settings before eliminating a person completely, especially if you share common friends or if there's the possibility of your running into each other in public.

· **Keep in mind that people will form opinions and judgments about you from the information you post on your wall or on your profile.** While everyone understands that you have a personal life (and a sense of humor), what may be clearly humorous in person may not come off as well when the context is missing. As the saying goes, "When in doubt, leave it out."

Twitter

· **No tweeting while meeting.** Be courteous to others by giving your full, undivided attention. If you want to tweet, do it when others aren't around.

· **Don't tweet in heat.** Cool down and think twice before sending a tweet when you're upset, angry, or frustrated. Nothing will be gained and much can be lost when you tweet in the heat of the moment.

· **Don't drink and tweet.** If you send a tweet while tipsy or intoxicated, it could tarnish your personal brand and your relationships with others.

· **Keep classified information private.** Need I say more?

· **Think twice before you tweet.** Twitter is a public medium and is visible to everyone. Sending the wrong tweet may get you fired, be used against you in court, diminish your chances of getting a job, or have other negative repercussions.

· **Remember that what's rude in life is rude on twitter.** Any comments that are mean-spirited or laced with criticism say more about the sender than the person in question. It's best to vent your frustrations in private to a trusted friend rather than use Twitter as an outlet.

CHAPTER 13

The Likability Factor

THREE THINGS IN HUMAN LIFE ARE IMPORTANT: THE FIRST IS TO BE KIND; THE SECOND IS TO BE KIND; AND THE THIRD IS TO BE KIND.

— HENRY JAMES, AUTHOR AND LITERARY CRITIC

My mother, who was a hairdresser by trade, had a thriving clientele, in part because she was so talented. But what really made Mom stand out was her gift for making her customers feel valued and appreciated while she washed, dried, cut, curled, colored, or styled their hair. Mom's greatest strength was her impeccable people skills.

Mom died in February 2009 and I miss her deeply every single day. Even though she's not physically with me, she still inspires and influences me in so many ways. I will always appreciate all the wonderful things she taught me—especially the meaning and execution of grace and kindness, including thoughtful ways to incorporate them in my daily life. She taught me the immeasurable importance of being kind to others, regardless of who they are or how much money they do or don't have, and always doing my best and believing in people's essential goodness.

Individuals with superb people skills will always top others in their field, regardless of whether they are hairdressers, physicians, electricians, or clerks. Perhaps it's occurred to you that people skills are often more difficult to learn than technical skills, but they're well worth the effort. If you have what I call the likability factor and you're well regarded, you will not only have more people on your side, but you will also have little trouble persuading them to stay there. Likability is one of the main reasons why we are drawn to do business with others and why we remain loyal to them.

People Skills Are Professional Skills

When most of us are faced with a choice to work with a Jerky Janet or a Friendly Fred, we almost always opt for likability over ability. The reason? When people like each other they connect, and good things happen when people who feel connected collaborate on projects. Tasks flow quickly, and everyone gladly pitches in. In most cases, when given the chance we choose our work partners based on two criteria: one is competence (does Fred know what he's doing?), and the other is likability (is Fred enjoyable and easy to work with?). Obviously both criteria matter, but it isn't always obvious just how important the second criterion really is.

When we need help getting a job done, we'll most likely choose a congenial colleague over a more capable but less cordial one. In a *Harvard Business Review* article titled "Competent Jerks, Lovable Fools, and the Formation of Social Networks" (June 1, 2005), Tiziana Casciaro and Miguel Sousa Lobo state that if someone is strongly disliked, his or her competence is almost irrelevant; people simply won't want to work with that person.

By contrast, if someone is well liked, colleagues will perceive that a higher level of competence may exist. Based on this finding, we might conclude that in the eye of the beholder an extra dash of likability is more desirable than a little extra competence.

If you would like to add an extra dash of likability to your skill set, here are the three essential attributes that engender credibility and likability in business and in life.

Empathy: Empathy is the ability to understand and view another person's situation through his or her eyes, and it's a core component for maintaining strong, enduring relationships. Empathy is a valued and often rare skill that requires self-awareness, experience, and practice, providing us with valuable insight into what other people are thinking or feeling. As I've gotten older, experiencing the ups and downs of life has helped me to have more empathy for others. For example, I can empathize with anyone who has lost a job, launched a business, had cancer, lost a loved one, met with financial struggles, or written a book.

When you and another person have been through a similar experience, you identify at a personal level. A bond connects the two of you, resulting in a shared level of trust. In both your personal and professional pursuits, empathy is the balm that keeps relationships running smoothly and produces measurable, positive outcomes. In a popular *Harvard Business Review* article titled "What Makes a Leader?" (January 1, 2004), psychologist and author Daniel Goleman writes: "Leaders with empathy do more than sympathize with people around them: they use their knowledge to improve their companies in subtle, but important ways." This doesn't mean that empathic leaders have to agree with everyone's view or try to please everybody. Instead, they "thoughtfully consider employees' feelings—along with other factors—in the process of making intelligent decisions." Obviously, empathy is an ability that is well worth cultivating.

Reliability: Thousands of businesses lose customers every day because employees don't live up to reasonable expectations of reliability, responsibility, or dependability. When we need a service, favor, or task performed by a set date, we are more prone to call on those who we are sure will deliver on their promises. If your air conditioner breaks in the middle of a sweltering summer, you don't want to wait days or weeks for someone to come and fix it. Or worse, if your toilet breaks in the middle of the night and starts to overflow, you don't want to wait a minute longer than necessary to get it fixed. You want the repair done, you want it done right, and you want it done right now.

Reliability means being able to count on someone, whether it's a company, friend, or family member; there's a sense of security in knowing we can get support in the moments that matter. Whenever I need a package delivered overnight, I use FedEx. Why? Because I have done business with FedEx for years and I know they will get my package where it needs to go and it's guaranteed to get there on time. FedEx might charge a little more than other shipping companies, but it's worth it for me to have peace of mind. Many companies have built their reputation by providing certainty (peace of mind) for their customers. This is true in the case of successful restaurants. If you visit a Starbucks, you know that the coffee will taste the same in Miami as it does in Milan. Reliability builds trust, trust forges loyalty, and loyalty means lasting relationships. In life, as in business, your most reliable connections often become your friends.

Integrity: Investor and philanthropist Warren Buffett once said, "In looking for people to hire, you look for three qualities:

integrity, intelligence, and energy. And if they don't have the first, the other two will kill you." I've always believed that you can buy intelligence and energy, but you can't buy integrity. Integrity is one of the most valuable traits a person can possess, and it's one that must be practiced every day. Integrity is doing the right thing (not necessarily the popular thing); it's saying what you mean as well as meaning what you say and doing what you say you'll do. Many people opt for keeping their mouths shut and "going with the flow" instead of standing up for what they believe or know is right. It's been said that integrity is doing the right thing when no one is watching, and yet in our culture too many people have the attitude of, "Everyone is doing it, so why shouldn't I do it, too?" as if that makes it justifiable.

A lack of integrity can be seen everywhere: politics, sports, the corporate world, and the entertainment industry. You'd be hard-pressed these days to find a TV show or movie that doesn't glorify deceit or dishonesty in some way. As the saying goes, follow the money. In other words, controversy or treachery sells tickets and boosts ratings. I agree with what Hal Urban writes in his book *Life's Greatest Lessons:* "If you genuinely want to succeed in life, honesty isn't just the *best* policy; it's the *only* policy." Certainly this speaks to professionalism in action.

Whether we're dealing with family, friends, coworkers, clients, or customers, no relationship can survive without all parties possessing integrity and honesty. Simply put, integrity means consistently applying our best judgment and highest level of behavior in all areas of our lives. At times this may be difficult, but in the long term it's certainly worth the effort. And the best part about cultivating integrity is that your personal investment of time, energy, and self-enhancement will pay you back in big dividends down the road.

Your success in the workplace is not guaranteed by your technical skills but by the way others perceive you and how well you relate to them. Credibility is the bedrock of likability. When you possess both of these valuable characteristics, you double the odds that others will want to do business with you. As a professional, how could you want anything less?

CHAPTER 14
Follow Through or Fall Back

I'VE LEARNED THAT PEOPLE WILL FORGET WHAT YOU SAID, PEOPLE WILL FORGET WHAT YOU DID, BUT PEOPLE WILL NEVER FORGET HOW YOU MADE THEM FEEL.

— MAYA ANGELOU, AUTHOR AND POET

Mary Kay Ash, the famed founder of Mary Kay Cosmetics, once said, "Those who are blessed with the most talent don't necessarily outperform everyone else. It's the people with follow-through who excel." The achievers in this world know that in order to make things happen, you have to follow up on your plans, promises, and next steps. It's sad but true that countless business deals and job opportunities are lost every day simply because people don't make the effort to follow through.

If you collect a person's business card, don't stick it away in a file or drawer; use it in a deliberate and thoughtful manner. Look for ways to regularly share information with those you've met, especially those you'd like to know better. Ask people their preferences for staying in touch, and then adjust your communications accordingly. Some people prefer e-mail, some like the telephone, while others might prefer text messaging, depending on their age and profession.

The key to cultivating business relationships faster and more effectively is being of service to those with whom you connect. In short, think "give" rather than "get." Read local business journals, industry publications, consumer magazines, or national newspapers with an eye out for articles that may interest friends, coworkers, colleagues, or customers. In no time at all, you'll become known as a "knowledge broker," someone who provides links, sources of information, and in some cases knowledge itself to organizations in a network. If you hear of an opportunity that might benefit someone else, share it. People are flattered when they know you are thinking of them and that you have their best interests at heart.

Some of my greatest business opportunities have come about as a result of my willingness to follow up. When my friend and former boss Dale Carlson invited me to be her guest at a bank-sponsored business luncheon, she immediately introduced me to the bank's public relations manager, Susie. When I told Susie that I was a local etiquette consultant, she mentioned that her company had hired an etiquette consultant several years ago to do some training on the subject. After several minutes of conversation, Susie gave me her card and suggested that I keep in touch.

As soon as I got back to my office, I wrote her a note telling her how pleased I was to make her acquaintance. I thanked her for the lovely luncheon and enclosed an autographed copy of my book *Business Class*.

Several months later, I received a surprise phone call from Susie's boss inviting me to meet with him to discuss possible training opportunities. I put together a proposal for his review, and he eventually hired me to train all of his wealth managers in Florida.

Professional success rarely, if ever, happens by accident. It must be intentional. In this case, my instinct to follow up paid off handsomely.

Five Ways to Make Yourself More Memorable

Now that you know that follow-up is vital to your career success, here are some surefire ways to make yourself stand apart from your competitors and become more memorable to others.

1. **Remember that follow-up is most effective (and impressive) if you contact a person within twenty-four hours of your meeting.** If you meet someone at a business luncheon, send an e-mail later that day. If you meet a client or colleague for dinner, send a thank-you note or e-mail the next morning. Out of sight leads to being out of mind, so if you don't stay in contact or make it a practice of supplying prospects and clients with helpful, usable information, you may quickly become a distant memory. By regularly staying in touch with your prospects and clients, you'll ensure they'll be far more likely to refer you to their friends, family, or associates rather than recommending your competitors.

2. **Ask new acquaintances if you can connect with them through one of your social networking sites, including LinkedIn, Facebook, and Twitter.** You may even want to enter their names and e-mail addresses and other perti-

nent information in a contact management program and then set up reminders to make contact on a monthly, quarterly, or bi-annual basis.

3. **Clip relevant articles or send links of interest to people in your network.** The operative word here is "relevant." The right message at the right time shows people that you're thinking about them and have their best interests at heart.

4. **Keep your word.** This is the hallmark of professionalism. The quickest way to damage your credibility, tarnish your reputation, and lose another person's trust is to ignore phone calls and e-mails. If you tell someone you will do something, make sure you do it. Don't keep people in limbo. Opportunities might vanish if your follow-through takes too much time. We live in a ramped-up, impatient, I-want-it-yesterday society, and your attention to detail and timing will go far with others. You build your professional credibility by delivering on your promises.

5. **Express gratitude.** Get in the habit of expressing your appreciation to those who share their energy, time, and resources with you by penning a handwritten note. We all love to read or hear those two magic words "Thank you." And while e-mail is a perfectly acceptable way to follow up, nothing makes a better impression (or can more effectively capture someone's attention) than a warmly worded note. A prompt, friendly thank-you note is an opportunity to repeat your desire to meet again and offer your help. If you're thinking that your handwriting is

messy and unreadable, either print or type your note, but
make sure to add a handwritten postscript and your signature to personalize it.

When you make follow-up a habit, it will become an auto-
matic part of your routine. The result is that your relationships
will soon become stronger, they will last longer, and your return
on investment (ROI) will slowly and steadily increase.

CHAPTER 15

Seven Unwritten Rules Every Professional Needs to Know

THERE'S A BASIC RULE WHICH RUNS THROUGH ALL KINDS OF MUSIC, KIND OF AN UNWRITTEN RULE. I DON'T KNOW WHAT IT IS. BUT I'VE GOT IT.

— RON WOOD, GUITARIST FOR THE ROLLING STONES

In the movie *A League of Their Own,* the character played by Tom Hanks scolds his right fielder, Evelyn Gardner, for bursting into tears. She had to learn a rule no one had ever bothered to tell her: there's no crying in baseball.

In the business world, some rules are officially recorded and easy to identify, but others, like baseball's no-crying rule, are nowhere to be found in any league or employee manual. Maybe in your first corporate job you asked yourself, *How does a person get to know the unwritten rules without violating one or more of them?* Well, that's a good question.

There are all kinds of unwritten rules in every workplace. They dictate how we should treat one another and work and play together (or not). A lot of the rules are learned through trial and error or from someone who knows the nature of the game. But you can always learn quite a lot by simply watching what others do or don't do and noting which behaviors are encouraged or frowned upon.

For some of us, discovering unwritten rules can take a while, but in Cathie Black's case she learned one rule right out of the starting block. In her book, *Basic Black,* she describes what happened shortly after she began working at *USA Today* when her boss, Al Neuharth, asked her to take part in a 9:00 a.m. meeting at Gannett's Madison Avenue office. In the book, she explains:

> I planned to get there a couple of minutes early, but my phone rang at 8:45 a.m. Neuharth's executive assistant, Randy Chorney, was on the line.
>
> "Cathie," she said, "where are you? The management meeting's about to begin."
>
> "I know," I told her. "It's at nine, right? I'll be upstairs in a minute." I hung up the phone, slightly confused, and hustled to the conference room on the thirty-second floor, a sleek, stylized, gray-walled chamber with black leather chairs and a U-shaped table. When I arrived at 8:51, everyone was already seated at their assigned spots, looking as though they'd been settled in for hours. As I took my seat, I shivered—it couldn't have been more than about fifty-eight degrees in that room.

This was Cathie's introduction to one of Mr. Neuharth's unwritten rules: "He liked to start meetings early, he liked to keep conference rooms chilly, and," as Cathie describes, "he liked to keep people a little off balance."

There are multitudes of implicit behavioral requirements (survival skills) that go along with learning about unwritten rules, and they have nothing to do with the technical aspects of a job. Corporate savvy is acquired with time and experience, and these skills are often taken for granted as "what the successful people know."

Many of us only learn the rules once we break them, but if you study your workplace and the people in it you can figure many of them out. Learning what behaviors you get reprimanded or rewarded for will not only work in your favor; it'll also help keep you out of trouble.

It's your advantage to be in the know so you're not taken off guard if you violate an unwritten rule. People who understand the culture know whom to associate with. They often end up with the plum projects and get promoted because they know how to make themselves virtually indispensable. This is a good goal to work toward as you progress in your career.

It may take time to crack the code of a person or company's unwritten rules, but if you study your surroundings and commit to keeping your eye on the ball you, too, will hit those home runs. Do the work and the pennant will eventually be yours. Here are seven universal unwritten rules I've learned from some of the world's most talented and professional executives.

Rule #1: Be Mindful of the Details

Some years ago, I was invited to meet the CEO of a large health-care company to discuss my business-etiquette programs. As the CEO spoke, I pulled a pen out of my briefcase and started taking notes. A few minutes later, he asked, "Where did you get that pen?" Quizzically I looked at my pen, and then I realized that it was imprinted with one of his competitors' logos! I'm sure he couldn't help but notice my "deer in the headlights" expression. Instead of making me feel smaller than I already felt, he chuckled and nonchalantly handed me one of his company pens.

This embarrassing incident taught me that little touches (such as having the right pen) count. Fortunately, the CEO felt that my professional prowess took precedence over the writing implement I used that day and he hired me to teach an etiquette program to his staff. Mistakes like mine can be avoided if you pay attention to the tiny details. If you don't, your potential client, customer, or colleague might wonder what else you might overlook.

Rule #2: Never Assume

When meeting with potential clients or customers, always connect with everyone in the room, regardless of gender, title, or authority level. Back in the old days, it was once assumed that men made a bulk of the buying decisions in their households; however, times have changed. Today, women account for more than 85 percent of all consumer purchases, including everything from automobiles to health care.

A few years ago, I was in the market to lease a new car, so I invited my husband, Brian, to come along for moral support. I had done the research and run the numbers and was prepared to negotiate for the car I wanted. As Brian and I sat in the sales manager's office to discuss the price and terms of the lease, the salesman primarily directed his answers to my husband and paid little attention to me. I ended up leasing the car because I got a great deal, but I never recommended that dealership to my friends. If a similar situation were to happen today, I would take my business elsewhere.

Times have changed. Companies that might have overlooked female buyers are now courting this key consumer. Even home improvement stores that marketed power tools and drywall solely to men are aggressively pursuing women by offering classes on how to make home repairs. Decision makers come in all forms and styles. In essence, that means if you treat everyone as if they're the decision makers, you'll increase your chances of winning the business.

RULE #3: HAVE A MEETING BEFORE THE MEETING

Children instinctively know how to have a meeting before a meeting. They know that by getting one parent to approve or agree upon an idea they increase the likelihood of the other parent following suit. As we grow into adulthood, we seem to forget this artfully devious yet effective technique.

To ensure that people are receptive to your idea, product, or service, schedule a meeting *before* the meeting. When you meet or have a phone conversation with an executive committee or a planning group prior to your scheduled meeting with other members of the group, it gives you the opportunity to get management's "buy-in." This way, they'll know exactly what you'll be doing, which will enable them to properly sell and promote you, your idea, or your product or service to their other team members. Doing this ensures a more successful outcome, and people will appreciate your level of professionalism.

Rule #4: Show Respect

Respecting people's privacy and presence should be a common practice in the workplace, but many people violate this rule. A lot of workers barge into each other's offices or cubicles, interrupt conversations or phone calls, and act as if they're entitled to immediate undivided attention. It's best not to assume that everyone you work with has an open-door policy. The respectful way to make an entrance is to knock or make eye contact and then wait until you're invited in.

If you're meeting a customer or a person of authority in his or her office, remain standing until you're directed where to sit, or alternatively ask, "Where would you like for me to sit?" If the answer is, "Sit anywhere," the unwritten rule is to choose a chair rather than a sofa. You'll be able to maintain your posture better if you're comfortably seated on a chair instead of being absorbed into a soft, cushy sofa.

Put your briefcase or portfolio on the floor next to you instead of placing it on a chair. You may not think the bottom of your case is dirty, but others might. Keep both feet on the floor. If you're a man, don't cross your legs in the figure four position. (This is when the ankle of one leg rests on the knee of the other leg). This could make you appear too casual or closed off. In some cultures, when you expose the sole of your shoe it's considered an insult.

Silence your electronic gadgets so you can stay focused on your discussion. If you absolutely must maintain constant access to your office or family members because of extenuating circumstances, explain your situation at the beginning of your meeting. If you have to take an emergency call, excuse yourself and step outside the room. Make it your own unwritten rule that when you meet with people you give them 100 percent of your time and attention. You'll be appreciated for your efforts, as this is so rare these days.

RULE #5: BE KIND TO EVERYONE

We will be judged by how we treat people who have less power or status than we have. Be nice to everyone you interact with and your kindness will come back to you in abundance. Show respect to the executive assistants, also known as "gatekeepers." They hold the keys to the kingdom, and most likely the boss places a lot of value on their opinions.

If you are waiting to meet with the decision maker, keep in mind that everything you do is visible (and sometimes audible, too). You never know who might be watching. Dora Vell, a managing partner of Vell Executive Search, a boutique executive search firm in Boston, Massachusetts, once worked for a company where the receptionist alerted partners if candidates didn't wash their hands after using the restroom. Her secret? She could hear the faucet from where she was seated!

Give every appearance of being patient and pleasant, especially if you're kept waiting. If you're offered a beverage, be cordial and accept it. If the assistant doesn't look extremely busy, use this extra time to make small talk and get acquainted. Comment on photographs and take note of any awards. If possible, find out the assistant's name and use it. Keep your conversation friendly and brief. You'll stand a good chance of being remembered the next time you call if you can bring up a subject the two of you discussed during your first visit.

Avoid overly familiar or potentially insulting terms such

as "hon," "sweetie," "babe," "dude," "son," or "guy." In short, a poised professional makes it a point to treat everyone with respect, from those in everyday service positions to VIPs.

RULE #6: BE PUNCTUAL

When you show up *on time* it sends a positive message to the person you're meeting with. It says, "You're important to me." Always give yourself extra time in case you get lost or have to maneuver through traffic jams, deal with parking hassles, or wait in long security lines or slow elevators. Get to your appointment at least fifteen minutes early so you can use the restroom, freshen up, or do whatever is necessary to be ready to present your most composed self. If you show up even three minutes late for a half-hour appointment, you may have ten percent less time to win someone over, and if you're ten minutes late you may have lost a whopping 33 percent. Punctuality pays off.

However, don't arrive too early. You don't want to catch your client or the person who will be interviewing you off guard. If you have too much waiting time, anxiety might mount. Find a coffee shop (drink decaf) or take a short stroll. These small yet important steps will help you feel more composed and poised than your competition.

RULE #7: CLEAN UP; DON'T COVER UP

Know your strengths, admit to your weaknesses, and most of all take responsibility for your behavior. If you make a mistake, admit it promptly and fix it before anyone else notices and sounds the alarm. In other words, clean up after yourself.

While we'd like to think that we can hide our mistakes, we really can't. But that's not the point. Dishonesty prevents us from being the type of person we can and want to be. I've seen first-hand how deception has created havoc for some of my own friends and family. Like a cancer, it starts small and, if it's not completely eradicated, can spread out of control. Dishonesty is costly; it kills relationships, causes undue stress, and can derail a career faster than you can say "train wreck."

Placing blame is equally destructive and almost guarantees an immediate loss of trust. When you own up to honest mistakes, you not only earn the respect of others but also become known as a person of integrity. Take comfort in knowing that the manner in which you acknowledge and repair a mistake can be every bit as important (if not more so) as a flawless work record.

CHAPTER 16

Listening: The Lost Link in a Loud World

THE OPPOSITE OF TALKING IS NOT LISTENING.
THE OPPOSITE OF TALKING IS WAITING.

— FRAN LEBOWITZ, AUTHOR

My good friend Bob Danzig is a motivational speaker, a bestselling author, a former CEO of Hearst Newspapers, and the best listener I know. Every now and then we get together and go for a walk on the beach. Whenever we're together, he makes me feel like I'm the only person in the world. What a rare quality to find in a friend these days. Bob asks me about my business goals and my upcoming projects, and then he offers his sage advice when I ask for it. I marvel at his gentle wisdom, and I find myself hanging on his every word.

After our walk, we usually go to a local café for breakfast. I love watching the way Bob's positive personality touches everyone he encounters. He always has an upbeat greeting for the server or cashier (or anyone else). He calls people by name and makes sure to tell them they're doing a great job.

Do you find yourself beaming inside when someone gives

you his or her kind, focused attention? I certainly do. But why don't more of us (myself included) extend this precious interpersonal gift more often? We're certainly capable of listening well when it *really* matters, but social graces can fly out the window when we're tired, preoccupied, or only marginally interested. What makes Bob Danzig stand out is that his warm attention and interest in others is so consistent; that's just the way he is.

Many people think of listening as a passive activity, but nothing could be further from the truth. Good listeners operate at a highly involved level; every part of them is intently engaged, especially their minds.

The former talk show host Larry King once said, "Here's what I remind myself every morning: Nothing I say this day will teach me anything. So if I'm going to learn, I must do it by listening." Communication experts consider good listening an even greater accomplishment than speaking well. Personally, I think that listening well takes a lot more energy than talking.

If you're on a first date with someone special or on a job interview with a prospective employer and you really want to impress this person, chances are you'll do everything in your power to appear interested and connected. You'll ask the right questions and pay attention to the answers as if your life depended on it. When you're on a sales call with a VIP client who represents a big sale (or a big commission), you would do everything possible to make a good impression by listening intently to what he or she has to say.

I like to ask my seminar participants, "What single standout quality makes a great boss or a great leader?" Without fail, "good listener" tops the list. We're all drawn to people who make us feel special, and being listened to is the one behavior that will do it for us every time.

Lead by Listening

The greatest managers I've ever known are excellent listeners. They connect with their employees (at every level) and ask for opinions. They actively seek input and take the comments, suggestions, and concerns they receive into consideration. Invariably, they only offer advice when it is solicited; in other words, they listen more than they talk. And when they do have something to say, it's often powerful and profound.

I once had a mentor who would say, "Never give advice or criticism unless you're being paid for it." Often, when people open up, they're not really looking for opinions or advice; they just want or need to be heard. I was once told that what separates extraordinary leaders from the ordinary ones is that the great ones work on their listening skills *all the time* and eventually everyone notices. If you want to be known as an effective leader, enhance your listening skills.

We may think we know how to listen, but few of us take it to a level of mastery. I'm sure you know what it's like trying to have a conversation with a coworker or boss who pays more attention to his or her paperwork or computer screen than you. Chances are you've had phone calls where the person on the other end of the line constantly types away during your discussion. How is it that these individuals don't understand how rude and dismissive they are?

When it comes to listening we want to offer our clients, customers, and coworkers the highest compliment that exists: our undivided attention. To accomplish this, use your eyes and ears so you can focus on the person in front of you. Close your office door if you have to. If you're on the phone, turn away from your paperwork, computer, or whatever you're working on and silence your cell phone.

· **Listen with your whole self.** Maintain eye contact without staring or glaring. Concentrate on the speaker and lean slightly forward to communicate that you are open to what is being said. Nod, smile, or ask a relevant question if you need clarification. This way, you send a nonverbal message that you are "in the moment" and fully involved in the conversation. Don't rush or hurry the exchange, be wholly and fully present, and you'll be long remembered for this.

· **Put your best face forward and smile.** A warm, genuine smile is the most beautiful curve on the human body. Your friendly expression says, "I'm approachable and interested," and it can immediately put others at ease. Researchers led by Ernest Abel* of Wayne State University in Michigan discovered that the "broader the grin and the deeper the creases around your eyes when you smile, the longer you are likely to live." The report goes on to read: "Those with the biggest grins had reportedly lived to an average age of 79.9—seven years longer than their straight-faced colleagues." When you smile during small talk you let people know you appreciate talking to them *and* you increase your longevity.

· **Open up and relax.** When we feel uncomfortable or threatened, we have a tendency to "fold up." We cross our arms, legs, or ankles. We might shift in our seat, put our hands in our pockets, or even angle our body away from others. These behaviors in effect "disconnect" or close you off from the person who is speaking. In Janine Driver's *New York Times* bestselling book, *You Say More Than You Think,* she writes: "The direction our belly button faces reflects our attitude and reveals our emotional state.

*Ernest L. Abel, Michael L. Krugar. "Smile Intensify in Photographs Predicts Longevity." *Psychological Science*, February 26, 2010.

When we suddenly turn our navel toward a door or exit or away from someone, we subconsciously send the signal that we want out of the conversation and perhaps even out of the interaction." Driver calls this *navel intelligence*.

· **Become aware of nervous gestures.** Nervousness manifests itself in many ways. It's natural to feel tense in certain situations, but if you want to socialize and meet people you should try to conceal your nervousness as best you can. Common signs of unease include fussing with your hair, jewelry, or clothing, adjusting your tie, clearing your throat every few minutes, repeatedly clicking a ballpoint pen, wiggling your foot, picking at your cuticles, and (gasp) biting your fingernails in public. My advice is to keep your body parts as still as possible without appearing stiff. Try to relax and take a few deep breaths.

· **Initiate contact.** If people don't seem to be approaching you, then take the initiative and be the first person to say hello. This demonstrates confidence and immediately shows your interest in the other person. As the conversation begins, nod, focus on what the other person is saying, and resist the temptation to interrupt or finish someone else's sentences.

· **Teach yourself to remember names.** Remembering people's names not only makes them feel good, but it also conveys respect. Some of us are better at remembering names than others, but research shows that we effortlessly remember those who are important to us. You increase the chances of remembering names if you repeat people's names as soon as they introduce themselves. Say their names periodically throughout your conversation. If you forget a name, don't fret. Instead, say something like, "It's been one of those days. Please tell me your name again."

· **Ask questions.** People perk up when we demonstrate a focused and sincere interest in them and their story. I was once taught that the two most powerful words when starting a conversation are, "Tell me." "Tell me, what is it you enjoy most about mountain climbing?" "Tell me, what are some of your favorite foods?" "Tell me, what are some of your favorite holiday memories?" If you take an active interest in the lives of those around you, people will remember and appreciate you for making the effort.

Make Listening a Professional Practice

As a rule, most of us would rather "do" than "just be." This means we'd rather speak than listen and express our opinions than listen to other people's viewpoints. This innate bias toward action can preclude us from being good listeners. Active listening, being fully present for the other person, can make you more memorable than you can imagine. The willingness to step outside of yourself and your concerns happens when wisdom, generosity of spirit, and compassion are combined with your intent to honor another human being.

"In the moment" listening is very much an art, and it is one of the most profound gifts you can give to others. My friend Bob Danzig is a perfect example of what happens when you are willing to shine the spotlight on other people by giving them your complete attention. When Bob walks into a room, people light up. With a little bit of work and a lot of the right attitude, you could do that, too.

PART FOUR

PASSION

CHAPTER 17

Rise and Shine

PEOPLE DON'T CARE HOW MUCH YOU KNOW UNTIL THEY KNOW HOW MUCH YOU CARE.

— JOHN C. MAXWELL, BESTSELLING AUTHOR AND LEADERSHIP EXPERT

Not only did my mother have an influence on my life, but so did her mother, Maitland Johnson. Granny Johnson was feisty, outspoken, and respected by everyone who knew her. Even though my grandmother had only a seventh-grade education, she possessed a great deal of wisdom. She used to advise all her grandchildren, "Be as good as the best, and better than the rest." I try to live and work by this philosophy each day.

In any highly competitive field—and these days every field is highly competitive—the only way to win is to be different and better than the rest. Yet, even though we've been advised to stand out in a crowd, it seems that most of us spend a tremendous amount of effort trying to blend in.

One person who knows the value of Granny Johnson's maxim about shining brighter and rising above the competition is Dino Wright. Dino is a master bootblack who has been polishing shoes for more than thirty years. He is the owner of Exec-U-Shine, based in Washington, D.C. Dino promises the finest shoe-polishing service in America, and he lives up to that promise because he knows that his job goes above and beyond the craft of shining shoes.

"I'm in the image enhancement business," Dino says with evident pride. "If I don't look good, it would be extremely difficult for me to convince my customers that I can enhance their image." Always dressed in a perfectly pressed suit, dress shirt, and silk tie, he caters to well-heeled lobbyists, lawmakers, and hotel guests at the Hyatt Regency on Capitol Hill. For six to eight dollars he can buff and shine a customer's shoes in five minutes or less. And although Dino touts his speedy and efficient service, he always tries to read his customers so he can gauge how long they want to sit in his chair: "Some use the time to relax and take a breather from their hectic day while others want a shine as quickly as possible."

In the metropolitan Washington, D.C., area, where there are plenty of bootblacks, Dino is well aware that good service is simply not good enough. He knows that to distinguish yourself from your competitors you've got to be the best, be different, or be both.

More important, Dino knows the value of providing operational excellence, which means that he provides his customers with reliable service at a competitive price and delivers it with minimal inconvenience and a little bit of flair. He creates customer intimacy by always thinking of ways to tailor his services to fit the needs of individual customers.

Dino offers a drop-off shoe service for people who don't have time to sit for a proper job. And for those who can't come to the hotel to see him, he will go to them. Yes, this remarkable man makes office calls—the ultimate in customer intimacy in a world filled with impersonal ways of doing business: "I go to the client's office and set up shop in a special area. Many of the employees bring in shopping bags full of their family's shoes that have been sitting in their closet for a very long time, and I make them look brand-new again."

Like any good entrepreneur, Dino looks at a customer's potential lifetime value to his company, rather than the value of any single transaction. He attributes Exec-U-Shine's longevity to his polished image, attention to detail, and willingness to offer his customers high-quality service in unique ways.

Home Alone

Another company that practices maintaining good customer relationships is Home Depot. I went there recently to buy a lightbulb. While I was in the lighting department, a clerk approached me.

"Do you have any questions?" he asked.

After I told him that I was looking for a particular type of halogen light, he spent fifteen minutes helping me find just the right size and wattage. He never seemed in a rush, and I ended up feeling as if I were the only customer in the store. He was genuinely interested in making sure that I received the right product, regardless of whether I spent forty-nine dollars or forty-nine cents. And what did he gain by spending all this time with me? A smile and a thank-you from a grateful customer (well, and having his story told in this book).

Individual service has become Home Depot's forte. Clerks spend time with customers because it's the nice thing to do, but more important, their company's business strategy is built around meeting the customer's needs for information and service. I received the right lightbulb *and* I became a little more educated about halogen lighting in the process.

A Step Above

When I shop for shoes, I always think of Nordstrom first. Why Nordstrom when I can get a similar pair of comparable quality for less money at another major department or clothing store? It boils down to the superior customer experience. You're pretty much guaranteed to have a positive experience whenever you make a purchase at Nordstrom. When I shop at other stores, I almost always have to wait until someone finally acknowledges me and often the salesperson doesn't fully understand my needs (or try to understand them). I'm sure you know the feeling. That's why so many of us are willing to pay a little more for a pleasant customer experience rather than having to almost fight our way through our purchase elsewhere for a lesser price.

In analyzing these three businesses, Exec-U-Shine, Home Depot, and Nordstrom, I've found that they share four common attributes:

1. **A Passion for Service:** Companies that truly value service are easy to spot. The positive attitude is everywhere: it starts with the first encounter and lasts until the transaction is over. If the business or a salesperson lacks a positive, upbeat attitude or demeanor, the transaction is doomed. But when someone has a pleasant can-do attitude that conveys, "I will do everything in my power to make sure that you have the best experience possible," not only will customers return over and over again, they

also will tell others about the incredible service they received. Talk about a win-win proposition, and all it takes is an attitude that says, "We deliver."

2. **Attentiveness:** No one likes to be thought of as just an account number or dollar sign. We all want to interact with someone who understands our unique needs and then customizes a solution specifically tailored for us. We also want someone who *listens* to us. When the salesperson at Nordstrom says to me, "You mentioned that you like a shorter heel, so I brought out another two pair of shoes with a similar style that you may not have noticed on the floor," I know she is listening to me. This is why Nordstrom is at the top of my list when I'm in the market for a new pair of shoes.

3. **Consistency:** Every time I walk into a Nordstrom or a Home Depot, anywhere in the U.S., I know that I'm going to receive the same level of world-class service regardless of where I am. From store to store and from department to department, the quality of service is consistent. Customers and clients love that. Service that is consistently dependable and reliable is something we deserve, and that's why we return to the businesses that know how to "do it right."

4. **Appreciation:** At the end of every purchase, the salesperson at Nordstrom carefully bags my items, walks around the counter, hands the bag to me, and then says. "Thank you for shopping with us." When Dino Wright finishes shining a person's shoes, he makes direct eye contact, flashes his million-dollar smile, and says, "I hope I see you

again, real soon." What's the cost of these niceties in terms of time? Thirty seconds? What is this type of service worth? Priceless!

If you act like everyone else or if your business looks like every other business, then all you've done is increase your pool of competition. Though our culture does a good job of touting the idea of rugged individualism, from the time we are children, we often travel in flocks, like birds, because blending in is the "safe" thing to do. We try especially hard to fit in when we want to get a job or work to win a client, and as a result we might tell others what we think they want to hear instead of taking a stand, being authentic, and telling the truth.

Fitting in with the crowd may work for a while, but eventually you will become predictable and, worse yet, maybe even dispensable. If you look and sound like everyone else, then why would someone be motivated to do business with you? Let what makes you different help you stand out from the pack. Take pride in your individuality and become adept at capitalizing on your uniqueness whenever and however you can.

As Italian actress and filmmaker Isabella Rossellini once said, "True elegance is the manifestation of an independent mind." What can you do, practice, or market that is independent of your competition? Think about the examples of small touches described in this chapter and how you might be able to separate yourself from the "flock."

Bestselling author and leadership expert John C. Maxwell once said, "Man does not live on bread alone: sometimes he needs a little buttering up." When you go above and beyond what is expected of you, you are giving your customers or clients the "butter." Remember that it's the butter, or the small touches, that separate the extraordinary person or company from the ordinary.

Remember my Granny Johnson's advice and challenge yourself to be "as good as the best and better than the rest." Figure out what your competitors aren't doing and then find a way to do it differently and better. Rise and shine: you'll be impressed with the results, because others will be impressed with you.

CHAPTER 18

Gratitude, Grace, and Acts of Kindness

**IT IS DIFFICULT TO GIVE AWAY KINDNESS.
IT KEEPS COMING BACK TO YOU.**

— CORT FLINT, AUTHOR

Throughout our lives, we all need something and someone to believe in. We also need someone who believes in us. That was the role my mother played in my life. I was once told that when you lose your parents you lose your fan club, and this is exactly the way I felt when my mom passed away. I can no longer pick up the phone and hear Mom's enthusiastic, "Good morning, Sunshine!" Nor can I call her for advice or tell her about my latest speaking engagement or TV appearance. No one will ever care about my success quite the way my mother did. And with each passing day I see myself becoming more like her as I try to keep her legacy alive through my words and actions.

Whenever I do something nice for someone else, I think of all the kind deeds my mother did for others—making soup for a sick neighbor, cutting and styling a friend's hair, and making tray favors for hospital patients. She loved practicing random acts of kindness long before that phrase was coined, and every day she looked for and welcomed opportunities to pass her generous gestures to others. My mother was grace in action.

Take Inventory

Mom believed that giving with gratitude is the secret to a successful life and career. She taught me that you must first find something you feel grateful for and then let yourself really feel it. Maybe you feel grateful that you have a wonderful job, that you work with people whom you like and admire, that you and your children are healthy and safe, or that you have a terrific marriage or partnership. Maybe you're grateful for the support you receive from a close friend or colleague. Maybe you're grateful that you have heat or air-conditioning in your home, a comfortable bed, and a pantry full of food.

Every night before you fall asleep, review what happened during the day that inspired feelings of gratitude. In the morning when you wake up, before you get out of bed, think of ten things in your life you most appreciate. If you're a visual person, make a "gratitude list" and write down the five things you most feel grateful for. Put the list on your bathroom mirror or on your refrigerator and look at it every day. Or better yet, carry it with you in case you have a frustrating moment and you need a positive reminder to get you back on track. Update it weekly or monthly. When you feel grateful it warms your heart and makes you want to share your emotional wealth with others through gestures of kindness or empathy.

Be a Practitioner of Good Deeds

Several years ago, a woman named Cami Walker from Hollywood, California, was diagnosed with multiple sclerosis, and the life she had known was about to change forever. Cami spent many days in and out of Los Angeles's emergency rooms with alarming frequency as she battled this perplexing neurological condition that left her barely able to walk.

Then, as a remedy for her condition, Cami received an uncommon prescription from a friend, an African medicine woman named Mbali Creazzo. Her advice to Cami was to give away twenty-nine gifts in twenty-nine days. "By giving," Mbali told her, "you are focusing on what you have to offer others and inviting more abundance into your life." Mbali told Cami that the gifts could be anything, but the giving had to be both authentic and mindful. At least one gift needed to be something Cami felt was scarce and valuable in her own life.

Cami was amazed by what unfolded during her monthlong journey. Many of her gifts were simple—a phone call, spare change, a cup of hot chocolate, even a facial tissue when a stranger was in need. Yet these acts of kindness were transformative.

By the twenty-ninth day of Cami's prescriptive program, not only had her health and happiness turned around, but she also had embarked on creating a worldwide giving movement. In 2009, she penned a book about her experience titled *29 Gifts*, which eventually became a *New York Times* bestseller.

Conduct your own experiment. Just for fun, strive to do something nice for others at work every day for twenty-nine consecutive days, and see if your relationships improve.

Share the Credit

Giving doesn't have to be in physical form; it can be a favor or kind gesture, a thank-you, a warm smile. It's amazing how much we like and admire people who are willing to share the credit, share the power, and share the glory. Some successful executives have reached a point in their careers where they are no longer willing to publicly recognize or give credit to those who helped them succeed. This is the quickest way to lose friends and allies and lose face. But when you share your positive feelings and express your gratitude to others, you give of yourself. Whenever you say "please" and "thank you" to the people who helped you accomplish your goals or a particular project at work, you pay it forward. Whenever you make a positive impact in someone else's life, no matter how small, you also make a positive impact in your own life.

Help Others

When you go to work each day with the intent to do something nice for someone, you create good karma. Everyone values the gift of unexpected assistance, and you never know when that kindness will come back to you many times over.

Derek Redmond, one of Britain's greatest athletes, competed in the 1992 Olympic Games in Barcelona, when his hamstring snapped in the four-hundred-meter semi-finals, knocking him to the ground.

As all the other runners raced past him, Redmond saw his Olympic dream vanish before his eyes. Determined to finish the race, Redmond struggled to his feet, fighting through the pain, and started hobbling toward the finish line.

Suddenly an astonishing thing happened. Derek's father, who was sitting in the stands, bolted out of his seat, dodged the security guards, jumped onto the track, and rushed to his son's aid. He put his arm around his son's waist and encouraged him to keep going. And as the crowd rose to their feet in applause, father and son made their way around the track to the finish line together. Redmond didn't win an Olympic medal, but with his father's help he managed to finish the race.

When was the last time you helped someone at work or in life accomplish a goal? People will admire you as a leader if they know that you will be there for them when they need you.

Let Your Attitude Drive Your Altitude

Did you know that your subconscious mind is like a computer that accepts whatever information you put into it? Author and teacher William Arthur Ward once said, "If you can imagine it, you can achieve it; if you can dream it, you can become it." What you think affects how you feel, and how you feel affects how you behave. When you program yourself to be grateful and have a good attitude it's like giving yourself an antidote against the negative influences that can potentially bring you down. In effect, you'll be looked upon more favorably when you choose to be positive, even when things don't go your way or when your plans go awry. You can tell a lot about a person by the way he or she reacts in times of adversity.

As you know, there is a lot of negative energy in many workplaces these days. But if you come to work each day with a cheerful and upbeat disposition, despite what might be happening in your personal life, others will respect and enjoy working with you. The same principle applies when you're making new connections. When you think positive thoughts, you exude positive energy, draw people toward you, and pave the way to new opportunities. By repeating positive affirmations such as, "This is going to be a good day," or, "I am finishing that project today," or, "I'm going to make an extra effort to meet three new people today," you're programming your mind for success.

However, if you engage in negative thoughts such as, *Oh, I hate Mondays,* or *I won't ever be able to start my business,* or, *No one is going to like what I have to offer,* or, *I can't stand my boss [colleague or client],* your actions (including your facial expressions) will mirror those thoughts and repel others away from you. It goes without saying that negative self-talk ultimately stands in the way of your success.

Bad attitudes are infectious. If you spend the majority of your time with people who lack vision or purpose and have no passion about their life or work, their apathy and lack of enthusiasm will rub off on you.

There's truth in the saying "If you want to soar with eagles, don't hang out with turkeys." If you want to connect with winners, seek out people who are the best at what they do. Befriend and spend time with those you most want to emulate. Any successful person will tell you that if you surround yourself with greatness, you can't help but become greater yourself.

A good attitude generates enthusiasm and initiative. Although no one really knows how to measure initiative or all that it entails, the willingness to do what needs to be done is one of the benchmarks of success. Initiative involves identifying a need or championing a solution for the benefit of others without being asked to do so. It's about seeing a need and going the extra mile—because it's the right thing to do.

Initiative is about taking the steps that make you, your company, clients, or colleagues just a little bit better. When you take initiative and do what needs to be done, your window of opportunity will widen. In other words, you'll be poised for success.

THE POWER OF PRAISE

For most people, the last bit of applause they may ever hear is when they graduate from high school or college. Every human being craves and *needs* praise, and it must be given appropriately and sincerely. When was the last time you said to someone at work, "You did a terrific job on this report!"? Or when did you last tell a coworker or administrative assistant, "I couldn't do my job as effectively without you. Thank you for all you do"? I believe that if we want to see the people in our lives respond like a thirsty plant responds to water, we should praise them whenever we can. When you give a coworker or colleague a sincere compliment you see him or her "fluff" up a bit and it's a great feeling to know you've made someone's day.

If you think of your subordinates as subordinates, it's time to pack up and find another job. But if you consider them your associates and treat them with dignity and respect, you'll always be held in good stead and they will work hard to make you look good. These people can make your life either easier or more difficult, depending on how *you* make them feel.

There is an old saying "Be careful who you step on while you're going up, because you'll be seeing those same people on your way down." Make it your job to build everyone up whenever you can. This is called leading by example, and it's a powerful practice that will come back to you time and time again.

CHAPTER 19

For the Health of It

**MY OWN PRESCRIPTION FOR HEALTH IS LESS
PAPERWORK AND MORE RUNNING BARE-
FOOT THROUGH THE GRASS.**

— TERRI GUILLEMETS, QUOTATION ANTHOLOGIST

Did you know that your level of performance at work is a direct reflection of the way you feel on both the inside and outside? Sure, stress is always going to be a part of our daily lives, but in order to be as competitive, poised, and successful as possible in today's world it's important to practice self-care.

Many people think that getting pedicures, choosing hand-dipped dark chocolates, and buying 600 thread-count bed linens equals self-care. But taking good care of yourself is not a form of self-indulgence. Self-care includes exercising regularly, eating healthy foods, getting enough sleep, pursuing creative outlets, and knowing how to relax and let go. All of this combined will help you perform better at work and in life.

At an intellectual level we all know that our bodies function better when we take good care of ourselves, but it's easy to take our health for granted, especially when we work a lot and take care of others. In my case, it took a major health scare for me to learn this all-important lesson.

When I left The Breakers and started my business over a decade ago, I was so consumed with the responsibilities and stress of starting a new business that I neglected to go to the doctor to get my annual well-woman exam. Four years breezed by before I decided it was time to go and get a checkup. Two weeks after I got my Pap smear my doctor called to tell me the bad news—I had cervical "adenocarcinoma in situ." I was diagnosed with the early stages of cervical cancer.

How could this be? I didn't have any symptoms or warning signs. Fortunately, the doctor caught it early enough, and I am cancer-free. Both my husband and I went through many months of stress and emotional duress that could have easily been avoided if I had taken better care of myself. But with every cloud in life there is a silver lining. My cancer experience taught me to take my job less seriously, to live in the moment, and appreciate the little things in life. But mostly, my brush with cancer taught me that when you face your hardship with mental hardiness you emerge from your struggle stronger, wiser, and more compassionate toward others who may be going through a tough situation.

It's so easy to put work ahead of others and especially yourself, but it's also detrimental to your health. If you don't have your health, you can't go to work. And if you can't go to work, you can't take care of your financial responsibilities. And if you can't take care of your financial responsibilities, you go bankrupt. You can prevent yourself from going mentally, physically, or emotionally bankrupt. Whenever you feel stressed out at work, remember to ask yourself, *Is this really worth putting my health at risk?* Learn to delegate, ask others for help from time to time, and take breaks when you need to. You're more valuable to others if you are healthy and happy instead of sick and tired.

Are You Sleepless in the Saddle?

Frank is a tollbooth operator who works the graveyard shift so he can take care of his aging mother during the day. Off-duty he complains that he is constantly sluggish and irritable. Frank is not alone. According to a 2008 National Sleep Foundation poll, almost a third of American employees report that daytime sleepiness interferes with their daily activities at least a few days a month. Those who work long hours report greater impatience, lower productivity, difficulty concentrating, lapses in memory, mood swings, and frequent sleepiness. And if that weren't enough, sleep deprivation impairs memory, weakens the immune system, slows metabolism, and, as some recent studies suggest, might foster weight gain.

Most experts agree that 8.5 hours is the optimal amount of sleep a person should have, but the average adult gets less than 7 hours per night. The negative effects of not getting enough sleep have led to $16 billion in annual health-care costs as well as $50 billion in lost productivity.

There are plenty of sleep-aid devices on the market, ranging from sound-soothing "white-noise" machines (yes, I have one, and I use it every night) and sleep apnea aids to mattresses covered in layers of silk, orthopedic pillows, and more. Prescription drugs are available, but as with many medications, they may merely mask the symptoms instead of treating the cause.

If you want to get more sleep, try to establish a bedtime ritual.

Try to go to bed at roughly the same time every night and give yourself a brief transitional period. Don't watch TV or work on your computer and then expect to conk out right away. It's also not a good idea to eat a big meal just before bedtime. Give yourself ample time to decompress from the pressures of the day. Keep the room cool and turn off any bright lights. Take a bubble bath or hot shower, light a candle, read, or sit quietly before you retire for the evening. Avoid alcohol for several hours before putting your head on that pillow; it may make you want to sleep, but you might wake up in short order and have trouble nodding back off.

Even a little additional sleep can help improve your performance at work, provide a better sense of overall well-being, and give you more enthusiasm for almost everything you do. It might even lead to more nighttime action of the intimate variety, too. That sounds like an aphrodisiac to me!

BECOME FABULOUSLY FIT

Naturally, you know that exercise is good for you—but do you know *how* good it is? People who exercise regularly are healthier overall and less likely to get sick. An executive who is physically fit is generally more resistant to the "bug going around" than someone who is not fit. Reduced absenteeism and reduced health-care expenditures are also the result of being healthier.

If you exercise regularly, you will have more energy and less stress, be more focused at work, and have a better attitude. Exercise can also increase your self-confidence and make you feel more attractive. In turn, this self-confidence empowers you to challenge yourself and strive for higher levels of achievement in the workplace.

Physical activity doesn't have to be drudgery. Two of my favorite workouts are yoga and the Latin-inspired dance-fitness program called Zumba. I enjoy yoga because it helps increase my flexibility, strength, and balance, and Zumba burns calories and helps with coordination. If I can't make time to go to the gym, I'll take a walk after dinner with my husband and our dog, which is an easy way to get in some family time and escape the pressures of the day. Find out what form of exercise best fits your lifestyle and then just do it. Any time you're moving and increasing your heart rate that's exercise, and it all counts!

PRACTICE PEACEFULNESS

We are a nation of "busybodies," rushing to and from work, dashing to the grocery store, going from one meeting to another, and even treating our meals as if they're timed events. Give yourself some quiet time each day. Make it a priority to stop whatever you're doing, shut down for a few minutes, and listen to that quiet little voice within you, your intuition. We are human *beings,* not human *doings.* Stop "doing" for fifteen or twenty minutes each day and just "be." This is difficult for most of us because we live in a culture that values being busy. Sitting and doing nothing feels unproductive, but this gives you a chance to recharge your batteries. Trust me, your body needs to relax. Every now and then give yourself a break, even if you have to begin with only two minutes at a time.

Get a Little Pet Therapy

There are numerous fascinating studies about the benefits pets have on their owners in terms of reducing stress, lowering blood pressure, and even helping them enjoy longer lives. More companies, particularly small businesses, are warming up to the idea of a pet-friendly workplace. A recent survey by the American Pet Products Manufacturers Association indicates that having pets in the workplace can create a more productive work environment, soothe corporate nerves, and decrease employee absenteeism. Companies that allow pets at work also experience improvement in employee morale.

Pets can also have a positive impact outside the workplace. Several years ago, I had the good fortune to take Oliver, my Cavalier King Charles spaniel, to Chicago with me. Whenever I travel alone on an airplane, I generally mind my own business and rarely go out of my way to talk to strangers. But when I travel with Oliver, there's no time to read, nap, or do much of anything else I usually do. This is because I'm kept busy answering questions from strangers such as, "What's his name?" "How old is he?" and "What breed is he?"

As Oliver and I were on our way back home from Chicago to West Palm Beach, we sat next to a young soldier on the plane who looked like he was in his late teens.

"Where are you headed?" I asked.

"Afghanistan," he replied solemnly. Be it fate or luck, I have a feeling that this soldier and I were meant to sit next to each other, because after several minutes of chatting with this young man he mentioned that he had a dog back home. He then asked if he could pet Oliver.

"Of course," I said.

During the two-hour flight, the soldier calmly and gently stroked Oliver's little head without saying a word. No words were necessary. For a brief period of time, the soldier's mind was no longer focused on the fact that he was about to go to war; he was focused on the unconditional love and goodness that only an animal can bring.

I am convinced that what we sometimes cherish in animal behavior is what we would like to see in humans. It's not often that we find a person who will love us without regard to age, status, income, physical appearance, or attitude. How many people do you know who always greet you with enthusiasm and are acutely sensitive to your moods? There's so much we can learn from our furry friends.

Remember, animals make people happy, and happy employees make customers and clients happy. In the final analysis, isn't this what every business owner wants for his or her company?

PASSION: FAKE IT UNTIL YOU FEEL IT

Did you know that having a positive disposition could have a powerful impact on your health as well as your relationships at work? The best part is that you can "force the issue" a little bit to keep yourself on the sunny side of the street. What I mean by this is, whenever you're not feeling particularly happy at work, try to fake it until you feel it. Smile, even if that's not what you really want to do.

If you want to feel more energetic, positive, or passionate, force yourself to act the way you want to feel. This is called as-if thinking. You pretend "as if" you are already happy. Would you like to be more positive, more in love with your life? Then behave as if you already are. Smile and suddenly you increase your face value.

In Jack Canfield's book *The Success Principles*, he writes about an exercise he does in his seminars called the Millionaire Cocktail Party. He invites all of his participants to stand up and socialize with one another as if they were at an actual cocktail party; however, they must act as if they have achieved all of their financial goals in life. He instructs them to act as if they have everything they want—their dream house, vacation home, dream car, and dream career—as well as having met any personal, professional, or philanthropic goals that are important to them.

I have tried this exercise in my seminars, and it's amazing to see the room's energy level soar. Everyone suddenly becomes happier, more animated, enthusiastic, and outgoing. People who seemed shy at first reach out and assertively introduce themselves to others.

When I stop the exercise and ask people to share how they are feeling, "Excited," "Passionate," "Happy," and "Self-confident" are common responses. I then remind the participants that their emotional and physiological states changed, even though in reality their circumstances were still the same. Even though they weren't actual millionaires in the real world, they had begun to feel like millionaires simply by acting as if they were.

You can begin right now to act as if you've already achieved any goal you desire as you learn to consciously manage your moods. You can't control outside circumstances, but you can control how you react to them. If you come home from work and your spirits are dragging, put on some happy music, watch a funny movie, read an inspiring biography—anything to make yourself smile or laugh.

When you give yourself an active dose of energy or enthusiasm (even when it's force-fed), your mood can't help but improve.

Health, like success in life and livelihood, doesn't just happen by accident. It takes purpose, passion, and daily practice. Remember, you're in charge. You are your own best energy source, capable of more than you know. Keep yourself healthy in mind and body, develop a millionaire mind-set, and who knows what you'll achieve? The sky's the limit!

CHAPTER 20

Fashion Your Life with Passion

**WHEN WORK, COMMITMENT, AND PLEASURE
ALL BECOME ONE AND YOU REACH THAT
DEEP WELL WHERE PASSION LIVES,
NOTHING IS IMPOSSIBLE.**

— NANCY COEY, AUTHOR AND SPEAKER

I believe that children have a valuable lesson to teach us and if you want to experience more wonder in your life, let a child take you on a tour of his or her world. Follow in a child's footsteps for a few hours, watch him or her play, and become a student of the moment. Remember what it's like to see the world through a child's eyes.

Ever since he was eight years old, my nephew, Austin, has always spent time with me during the summer. Each year when he arrives, I ask the same question: "What do you want to do while you're here?" His reply is always the same: "Play at the beach!"

Austin's visits are all about playing. We eat, watch movies, walk the dog, and go to the beach, where we throw ourselves at the ocean waves, build sand castles, and wear ourselves out.

If you ask an adult, "What do you want to do today?" what are the chances that you'll get the response: "Let's play!"? Maybe that's why so many people in our society are so stressed, uptight, and unhappy: we've lost our spontaneity.

Physician and author Oliver Wendell Holmes once said, "We don't quit playing because we grow older; we grow older because we quit playing." I agree. In the workplace, play can be a tool that smart leaders use to bring out the best in people. Playing together builds trust and morale, fosters more civility and kindness, and strengthens relationships between employees.

Here are just a few ways you can incorporate play into the workplace.

• Organize the all-purpose potluck luncheon to celebrate birthdays of the month or holidays.

• Remember that friendly competitions can be appropriate for the right circumstances. Organize softball, tennis, soccer, or bowling tournaments and other team challenges.

• Since volunteerism can be a great way to incorporate play, use it to make a positive impact in your community. Set a specific day each week or month and allow staff to volunteer for the charity of their choice. Have them report back the next business day and tell what they learned.

If you use your imagination and do your homework you can make play a common and useful occurrence in the workplace.

MAKE TIME FOR PLEASURE

No matter how successful we are in our careers, we human beings are still social creatures who yearn for a deeper connection within ourselves and with others. Unfortunately, many of us don't make time for fun and friends amid the frantic pace of our work life.

The good news is, striking a balance between work and life isn't as hard as we might make it out to be. We just need to identify and make time for a few activities that really matter to us. These activities are what I call soul activities. Soul activities bring satisfaction and joy to your heart. And when you feel more satisfied and happy, you are kinder and more polite to yourself and to others at work.

Treat a special client to a wine tasting, or ask a colleague to attend a cooking or dance class with you. Invite coworkers to go with you to take bags of candy to residents at a nursing home; get a group together and go for a hike, bike ride, or some other fun activity. Any of these activities can be considered soul activities as long as you're having a good time with someone else.

SPEND QUALITY TIME WITH YOURSELF

One of my favorite books is *The Artist's Way* by Julia Cameron. In it Cameron explains the importance of taking yourself on a weekly artist's date. An artist's date is similar to a soul activity except you do it alone. Create a day, a half day, or even an hour during which you give to yourself and not to anyone else. By committing to this, you have special time in which to replenish your spirit so you can continue to give to others without resentment or a sense of obligation.

If you're a workaholic (and even if you aren't), you'll be surprised to discover how your productivity and creativity will increase when you take artist's dates. It's rewarding to discover that when we allow even the slightest bit of positive inflow we are rewarded with an increase of creative outflow.

I love taking myself on artist's dates to bookstores, on beach walks, and to movies. Sometimes I'll treat myself to a massage. I don't always come away from my expeditions with a new conscious sense of creative direction, but I do, however, come away with a renewed sense of well-being and connection.

Sign up for an occasional community education or college course, either for pleasure or to enhance your professional development; stretch your comfort zone and learn a new language; or take up a musical instrument or sport. Play soccer or basketball after work, go to a museum, or take an art or music class.

For most of us taking the time for an artist's date is a matter of psychological and spiritual survival. If we don't do this for ourselves, we risk being sucked dry by everyone and everything that needs us. So my advice is that it doesn't matter what you do or where you go, just go!

Cultivate Creative Manners

It's when you're creative—when you do the unexpected, the unnecessary, the unasked for, and the imaginative—that the recipients of these acts of kindness really love you for it. Good manners and creative manners are not the same thing. Let's suppose one of your coworkers gets sick and has to go to the hospital. Good manners decree that you mail a get-well card to him or her. Creative manners mean that you send the patient some balloons and attach them to a beautiful plant or organize a group photo of everyone in the office and ask everyone to sign the mat that goes inside the picture frame.

Creative manners mean that you go above and beyond what is expected of you in any given situation. It is imaginative and requires a little bit of thought and preparation. I'm always amazed that some of the busiest people I know are the ones who always find time to extend a hand of friendship, make a phone call, or send a thoughtful card. They always manage to find the time to make others a priority in their lives.

Thinking about other people is the best reason I know for people to like you, to want to do business with you, and to become and stay friends with you. People who are preoccupied with themselves and their own problems score very low in popularity, but people with creative manners are admired and rewarded for their efforts, even though they expect nothing in return. In a nutshell, this is what being poised for success is all about. When you practice creative manners, you are making a contribution—to your friends and family, to your company, to your community, and most important, to the world.

ACKNOWLEDGMENTS

Actress and singer Doris Day once said, "Gratitude is riches." I believe this statement is true, because I have a wealth of appreciation for the many extraordinary individuals who helped make this book a reality.

Rita Rosenkranz, you are more than my literary agent—you are a friend, a comrade, and my staunchest advocate. Your patience, guidance, encouragement, and tenacity were vital in shepherding this book from conception to fruition, and I've thoroughly enjoyed sharing my literary journey with you.

I am so fortunate to have friends who are gifted writers and who agreed to generously give constructive critiques. Foremost among these is Marilyn Murray Willison—Marilyn, I appreciate your willingness to meet with me each week to brainstorm and help polish this diamond in the rough into a gem of a book.

C. Leslie Charles is a wordsmith par excellence—you have the uncanny ability to make any manuscript sing, especially mine. Words cannot express how much I appreciate your creativity, dedication, and passion. Thank you for encouraging me to put my heart on paper.

I'm indebted to the talented team at St. Martin's Press. I am especially grateful for Alyse Diamond, Kathryn Huck, Nadea Mina, Laura Clark, Paul Hochman, Barbara Wild, Jason Ramirez, Kate Ottaviano, Mariann Donato, and Dana Trocker.

Although I've been writing and speaking on business-etiquette topics for more than a decade, I found it helpful to call on wise friends for guidance and feedback. For this book I turned to Lauren Vitalie, Susan Bigsby, Brian Lipstein, Tom Grant, Andrew C. Petersen, Mark Spivak, Randall LaBranche, Kenny Sturgeon, Robert Hickey, Dora Vell, Dorothy Waldt, Bernardo J. Carducci, Ph.D., and Nancy Holder. Thank you so much for your valuable content and helpful suggestions.

Jorie Scholnik, my brilliant associate—you were always willing to carve out time from your busy teaching schedule to help research many of the topics in this book. You bring more than diligence to each project; you provide a refreshing, youthful perspective to some of the more time-honored etiquette principles that I speak and write about.

I owe a special thank-you to the many Facebook friends, blog readers, and Twitter followers who agreed to be the best focus group ever and for providing useful, candid, and timely feedback whenever I requested it.

Most of all, a giant hug and kiss goes to Brian Gleason, my husband and life partner—thank you for your love, support, and willingness to make the meals and keep our home intact during my many hours of book writing. I must also thank Oliver, my loyal Cavalier King Charles spaniel, for the long hours of companionship and for nudging me to eat, stretch, and take breaks.

And if you are holding this book and reading its pages, I'm thankful for *you*. My wish is that you will enjoy its contents and glean some insight and inspiration to become more poised for success.